W9-BUA-310

The Shield and the Cloak

GARY HART

The Shield and the Cloak

The Security of the Commons

OXFORD
UNIVERSITY PRESS

2006

OXFORD
UNIVERSITY PRESS

Oxford University Press, Inc., publishes works that further
Oxford University's objective of excellence
in research, scholarship, and education.

Oxford   New York
Auckland   Cape Town   Dar es Salaam   Hong Kong   Karachi
Kuala Lumpur   Madrid   Melbourne   Mexico City   Nairobi
New Delhi   Shanghai   Taipei   Toronto

With offices in
Argentina   Austria   Brazil   Chile   Czech Republic   France   Greece
Guatemala   Hungary   Italy   Japan   Poland   Portugal   Singapore
South Korea   Switzerland   Thailand   Turkey   Ukraine   Vietnam

Published by Oxford University Press, Inc.
198 Madison Avenue, New York, New York 10016

www.oup.com

Oxford is a registered trademark of Oxford University Press

Library of Congress Cataloging-in-Publication Data
Hart, Gary, 1936–
The shield and the cloak : the security of the commons / by Gary Hart.
p. cm.
ISBN-13 978-0-19-530616-3
ISBN 0-19-530616-3
1. National security—United States.   2. United States—Military policy.
3. United States—Foreign relations—2001–   4. United States—Politics and
government—2001–   5. World politics—21st century.   I. Title.
UA23.H36415 2006
355'.033073—dc22   2005028322

9 8 7 6 5 4 3 2 1

Printed in the United States of America
on acid-free paper

The social progress, order, security, and peace

of each country are necessarily connected

with the social progress, order, security, and peace

of all other countries.

—Pope John XXIII,

*Pacem in Terri*s (1963)

Preface

Two historic events, the end of the Cold War and the terrorist attacks on September 11, 2001, fundamentally altered the nature of national security and how to achieve it. The first eliminated the threat of nuclear attack from the Soviet Union. The second demonstrated America's vulnerability to a kind of savagery never seen in our country's history.

Taken together, these events present us with a threat and an opportunity. The opportunity is to redefine America's role in the world. The threat is to the security of our national soil. Currently, we are misusing the opportunity by waging preemptive warfare in the Middle East and thus possibly increasing the threat. The confusion arises from our attempt to apply an old understanding of national security to an entirely new world.

In a previous book, *The Fourth Power: A Grand Strategy for the United States in the Twenty-First Century* (Oxford University Press, 2004), I argued for a new grand strategy for the United States in the post–Cold War world that applied our traditional economic, political, and military powers to the achievement of three large purposes—

achieving security, expanding opportunity, and promoting liberal democracy. I further argued that we possess a fourth power, the power of the principles embedded in our constitutional system and our founding purposes, that gives us leadership stature in the world, but only to the degree that we live up to those principles ourselves.

In *The Fourth Power*, I suggested that a larger understanding of security than that of the Cold War was required to respond to the new realities of the twenty-first century. Those revolutionary realities include globalization, information, the erosion of national sovereignty, and the changing character of conflict. That larger understanding of security, I argued, is also required to encompass energy security, environmental security, the security of the community, and the security of livelihood.

In this book, I explore what security means in this new age, above and beyond sheer military power, and propose specific military and nonmilitary ways in which we might go about achieving it. The first step in this process is to think differently, to think anew, in Lincoln's words, to disenthrall ourselves from the simplistic, unilateralist notion that true security can be achieved merely by spending more money on weapons and by invading more countries.

As a product of the twentieth century, I understand the political inclination to see security in exclusively military terms. World War II was one of my first memories. A large number of members of my family participated. In many ways, we all participated. And the Cold War confrontation with communism was the central reality of most of my life. Consequently, when I was elected to the U.S. Senate, I joined the Armed Services Committee. For twelve years during the heart of the Cold War, I participated immediately and directly in virtually all the issues related to national security.

I studied naval warfare and strategy. I helped to found the Military Reform Caucus in the U.S. Congress which proposed a sweeping series of changes in personnel policies; bold departures in strategies, tactics, and doctrine; and dramatic changes in weapons procurement.

Many of those reforms are now being adopted almost twenty-five years later. I served on the first congressional committee to investigate the Central Intelligence Agency and uncovered, among many other un-American activities, CIA plots to assassinate Fidel Castro using major Mafia figures. Thereafter, I served as a charter member of the follow-up Senate oversight committee that prevented further abuses by our intelligence agencies.

I was particularly involved in arms control matters, including observing and participating in SALT (Strategic Arms Limitations Talks) and START (Strategic Arms Reduction Talks) negotiations in Geneva between the U.S. government and the Soviets. I studied issues such as "throw weight" (size of warheads) and "circular error probable" (accuracy) and listened to the nuclear priesthood discuss ways to conduct limited nuclear wars. I talked personally to Russian leaders in Moscow and, after lengthy discussions with President Mikhail Gorbachev in early December 1986, concluded that the Cold War was finally coming to an end, which it did shortly after I left the Senate. A large part of my decision to seek national leadership in the 1980s was to hasten that day so that my children's generation could be more secure than mine.

Most recently, I was co-chair of the U.S. Commission on National Security for the Twenty-first Century. This was the most comprehensive review of U.S. national security since 1947, and it took almost three years. As early as September 1999, our commission predicted catastrophic terrorist attacks on America, and in our final report in January 2001, we warned the new president, George W. Bush, that this terrorist threat was sufficiently imminent to require a massive reorganization of the U.S. government to prevent such attacks. Nothing was done, our warnings were ignored by president and press, and eight months later more than three thousand Americans died. For this utter neglect, no one has been held accountable.

My preoccupation with national security is far from recent; indeed it has spanned three decades. It is the basis from which I argue that the meaning of security must be more comprehensive today than it was in the previous century. There is an old saying that if you cannot solve a problem, make it bigger. By expanding the nature of security, I hope to make it more achievable.

In the Hilary (winter) term of 2005, I had the honor of being Visiting Fellow at All Souls College, Oxford, where the manuscript of this book was written. For their most warm and cordial hospitality, I owe a debt of deep gratitude to Warden John Davis and the Fellows of this extraordinary college.

In this effort, I have to thank a number of people: Jerry Cohen, Joyce Appleby, Jim Fallows, Bill Shore, Marcia Johnston, among others, for their critical and constructive review of this manuscript. And most of all, I wish to thank, once again, a superb editor, Dedi Felman, at Oxford University Press. She continues to ask the right questions.

Contents

The Shield and the Cloak

Introduction

The New Three-Dimensional Chess Game

Imagine the twenty-first century as a three-dimensional chess game. One dimension represents the United States. One dimension represents the world of nation-states. The third dimension—a new one—represents stateless nations.

In the twentieth century, national security was mostly two-dimensional. The United States and its democratic allies, the white pieces, faced off against other nation-states—imperialist, fascist, or communist—the black pieces. The democratic nations, the white pieces, prevailed because our pieces together were more powerful and, in most cases, we moved them more cleverly. In the twentieth century, security was achieved by the clever positioning of powerful forces according to the rules of the traditional, two-dimensional game.

As of 9/11, a new third dimension, stateless nations, was forced onto the security chess board. Stateless nations, or "nonstate actors" as they are called, do not play with the same figures or pieces. No knights in uniform. No rooks sheltering established national wealth. No kings and queens enthroned in national capitals. They also will not participate on the old two-dimensional chess board. Most of all, they refuse to play by the rules. So, security cannot be achieved in this new century by using the same pieces, even if you increase their size and power, and playing by the old rules.

Security can *only* be won by creating imaginative new pieces, deploying and maneuvering them much more creatively and swiftly, and consolidating the forces of the traditional two dimensions into a global commons—a figurative arena in which our collective security interests are deployed for the common good. We must also be willing to welcome new players, for example, by engaging China as we have in containing the North Korean nuclear threat, and to use our collective genius and wisdom to create new security rules for this new multilayered global chess game.

Our knights, our military forces, must look different, for example, like the Delta Forces in Afghanistan, and be trained and equipped differently. Our wealth must be brought out of its protective national castles and invested more wisely in mastering new sciences and technologies to reduce threats of climate change and pandemics. Our kings and queens, political figures out of touch with twenty-first-century realities, must be replaced by leaders smart enough to fully understand the new dimension and bold enough to define new rules for the new game. It also would not hurt if our bishops, our religious leaders, played a more enlightened and constructive role.

The new security will be both national and international, defensive and offensive. It will require a shield—and spear—representing new kinds of military forces, as well as a cloak that protects the global commons from nonmilitary threats. The old security required containing the Soviet Union within its borders. The new security requires a shield protecting the homeland from terrorists' threat and a spear to pin the terrorists in their caves.

The old security required cooperation among Western armies. The new security requires cooperation among intelligence services.

The old security required massive weapons in massive numbers. The new security requires special forces, individual warrior teams, searching for terrorists in tunnels and caves.

The old security required economic dominance. The new security requires economic integration in a world of international markets, trade, and finance.

The old security meant prevention of nuclear war. In addition to that goal, the new security is a cloak composed of security of livelihood, security of energy, and security of the environment.

This book proposes a new strategy of the commons that includes major reforms of our conventional military forces, specific steps to increase homeland security, a profound shift in economic priorities from consumption to production, the creation of an elite human intelligence corps, a new fifth special forces service, urgent reductions in the Russian nuclear arsenal, an international peace-making force, and many other proposals that are meant to be interrelated and intertwined.

Two new approaches are proposed here: One is the notion that genuine security now requires military (shield) and nonmilitary (cloak) components; the other is that security can only be assured through international cooperation. Most important, this book recognizes that security in the twenty-first century is an entirely new and larger concept than it was in the era of the Cold War. Perhaps no event in recent times illustrates this truth more vividly than the massive natural assault on the U.S. Gulf Coast, and the resulting insecurity, caused by Hurricane Katrina in late August 2005.

A confluence of revolutionary tides at the beginning of the twenty-first century is massively altering the strategic environment. These tides will require the United States to accept a new idea of national and personal security, one that embraces protection against terrorism, a shield, and one that includes protection against economic hardship, environmental harm, and energy wars, a cloak. This reality demands a profoundly different approach to security than we used in the most recent era.

My generation was bred to the challenge of security but in its former two-dimensional framework. As children of the last world war, we gained our maturity during the arms races, missile crises, and third world confrontations of the Cold War. "The Russians are coming," we were told, "and they are thirty feet tall." Never mind that they had no fleet to transport themselves to America's shores. One way or the other, they were out to get us. The threat was the idea, and the idea became the reality.

Our nation had to be made secure, and security was the product of strength. Strength was measured almost exclusively in military terms—numbers and sizes of missiles, warheads, tanks, ships, and planes. One central organizing principle dominated the foreign and defense policies of the United States and most of its allies during the second half of the twentieth century—containment of communism. This principle had the enormous appeal of clarity and brevity. *Containment* meant to keep communism from spreading beyond the Iron Curtain. And we all knew what *communism* meant— godless, totalitarian, and treacherous. Security in the Cold War was almost exclusively the shield of military presence under which economic competition was played out, but this shield was deployed far from the United States.

The Cold War lent itself to the kind of thinking most Americans admire and prefer: direct, straightforward, unambiguous, and black and white. Though not apparent at the time, in hindsight the Cold War had its traditional, two-dimensional appeals. We knew who the enemy was, and we often forced unrelated local conflicts into this two-dimensional mold, and we knew what had to be done. To be secure, communism had to be contained. It provided a comprehensive world view, one that suited us and one that we sought to impose on the rest of the world, including, in places like Vietnam, where it did not exactly fit. Such debates over security as there were occurred on the margins and focused primarily on numbers of troops and kinds of weapons.

Security, in its broadest sense, was understandable as much as anything else because it was played on the traditional chess board of great-power politics. We could not permit communism to expand in Asia, Africa, Latin America, or the Middle East. Otherwise, there was no stopping it, and we would be next. "Better fight them over there than over here" summarized the conviction of the person in the street and many politicians—and is echoed in the rhetoric supporting the Iraq war even today. We had let imperialism in Asia and fascism in Europe operate unimpeded for too long, and it cost all of us a lot of lives to crush them. We would not make that mistake with communism.

Two events occurred almost exactly a decade apart that changed all that. They marked the end of one kind of century, featuring the exclusively nation-state chess game, and the beginning of a totally new era. At the end of August 1991, the Soviet empire collapsed, and the strategy of containing communism became redundant. Ten years later, almost to the day, suicidal al Qaeda members destroyed an emblem of American capitalism and attacked the symbol of American military power. In that historic ten-year period, America made a crucial mistake, and we paid for it. We did not understand how profoundly the world was changing, that a new dimension had been added to the chess board, and therefore we did not forge a new understanding of security and how to achieve it.

Now, we must make up for lost time. Now, we must start at the beginning to understand security. But until we know what security means in this three-dimensional world, we cannot know how to achieve it. President George W. Bush has offered his substitute for the containment of communism. It is war on terrorism. Having defined his objective, he has offered his method—preemptive, even preventive, warfare. Though these are concepts known in international law, these are new doctrines for the United States. Justification for preemptive war requires a threat to national security that is "immediate and unavoidable." Preventive war, an even more dubious undertaking, simply involves attacking or invading another nation, even without an imminent threat, as a means of restraining or obstructing a theoretical or potential threat. Both preemptive and preventive war assume an almost infallible level of intelligence—namely, that weapons of mass destruction exist and, with a high degree of probability, they are going to be used—a degree of intelligence precision not demonstrated by the United States in recent times.

Most important, by using traditional military power against a largely new third-dimensional threat, we are inviting a stand-off at best and defeat at worst.

Both communism and terrorism might be evil. But communism was a rational evil, and terrorism—not an ideology propounded by a state—is irrational, suicidal evil. Rational evil might be contained. Irrational evil, according to this logic, must be eliminated by acting against states, in this case Iraq, which have been pronounced to be actual threats. But, as "nation-building" in Iraq is proving, a stand-off there may be the best we can achieve.

Those dissatisfied both with the current administration's limited understanding of security's new dimensions and its unilateralist and preemptive prescription for achieving security have a duty to produce a more comprehensive definition of security, the threats to it, and the methods of defeating or eliminating those threats.

An idea of security that provides both a shield and a cloak first requires that we understand our age, the new age of the twenty-first century. The new century is revolutionary, and it is revolutionary on multiple levels. First, there is globalization, or the internationalization of business, finance, and commerce. This really means the destruction of national barriers to trade in resources, products, and services. While creating new jobs and new opportunities, this revolution is undermining the authority of governments or states to control their own economies. Central banks, finance ministries, and treasury departments can no longer depend with certainty on traditional fiscal and monetary policies to stimulate economic growth or dampen speculative investment and therefore cannot guarantee control of their own national economic destinies to the degree they have in the past. There is a largely unregulated international financial market all around us that is running, so far, pretty much on its own.

As if globalization were not a huge enough revolution, and it is historic and epic by any standard, it is accompanied by an equally profound social and economic transformation called the information revolution. The computer chip and microprocessor are changing whole economies and societies at least as profoundly as did the industrial revolution of the early nineteenth century. The ways in which we work, learn, and communicate have altered stunningly in the past two decades and will continue to do so. Like globalization, information technology strengthens the capability of the state to intrude on citizen privacy, but it also transcends the authority and sovereignty of the state by giving citizens much more access to information, including secret information, than they ever have had before.

The respected strategic thinker John Steinbruner observed these trends and understood their implications some years back:

> If basic manufacturing and the provision of services are
> eventually driven to global scale to the extent that is
> technically feasible, then a progressively integrated
> international economy will emerge with properties that
> diverge sharply from past experience. . . . The national
> identity of all economies would also be diluted as the
> leading entrepreneurs adapt to the imperatives of
> organizing across cultural divisions. National govern-
> ments would not be able to prevent these effects without
> disrupting economic performance, nor would they be
> able to stimulate or regulate economic performance by

the standard methods of macroeconomic management. Since a spontaneously integrating international economy would generate universal incentives and require international operating rules, it would drive national governments into ever more intricate forms of collaboration in an effort to pursue national economic objectives. It also would disperse access to products, information, and technology of all sorts—some of them distinctly dangerous—and would intensify interactions among separate cultures. In general it would tie everyone's fate to everyone else's to an extent never experienced before.[1]

The net effect of these integrating trends is to erode state sovereignty, the third revolution. Then, the ability of the nation to appeal to the loyalty of its people begins to decline, and soon the state itself collapses. Max Weber is known to have said that the state begins with a body of armed men. The armed men provide security for their fellow citizens in exchange for their loyalty to the state. The twenty-first century now witnesses the revolution of failed and failing states, especially states artificially or arbitrarily formed many decades ago by European colonial powers, in parts of Asia, the Middle East, the Balkans, Africa, and isolated parts of South America. Iraq happens to be one of this number. Ethnic separatism and tribalism sprang up almost within hours of the disappearance of the Cold War. A century of political ideology has given way to a century of ethnic nationalism, religious fundamentalism, tribal separatism, and the rise of violence carried out by so-called nonstate actors. *Nonstate actors* in this context is simply a term of art used by foreign policy analysts to mean tribes, clans, gangs, and mafias. When the "armed men" representing the state can no longer guarantee security against treach-

---

1. John D. Steinbruner, *Principles of Global Security* (Washington, D.C.: Brookings Institution Press, 2000), pp. 7–8.

ery carried out by nonstate actors, citizens lose confidence in their government.

Under these circumstances, the state, in an attempt to shore up its sovereignty and its claims on citizen loyalty, often suspends liberties and consolidates its power. But, since the end of the Cold War, in most instances, for example in Ukraine, these last-ditch, desperate efforts are overwhelmed by popular democracy.

The transformation of war and the changing nature of conflict represent the fourth revolution. Except for the war on terrorism being conducted by the United States in Afghanistan and Iraq, the destruction of the past decade has been carried out by ethnic and religious warriors in Bosnia and Kosovo, separatists in Chechnya and elsewhere, tribal leaders in Somalia, gangs in Haiti, drug cartels in Colombia, and mafias in downtown Moscow. Even in Afghanistan, our immediate enemy was al Qaeda, a terrorist cabal, and we took down the Taliban government that harbored it. All of these conflicts represent a kind of violence much more characteristic of the eleventh-century Assassins than the clash of mighty national armies in twentieth-century world wars.

Thus far, then, the early twenty-first century is an age of global trade, tidal waves of information, failed and failing states, and wars involving tribes, clans, and gangs. The implications of all these revolutions are immense, not least for an understanding of security and how to achieve it. The shield provided by more missiles and missile defenses, larger traditional armies with larger weapons, more giant aircraft carriers and great battleships, and ponderous long-range artillery is not going to guarantee security in this revolutionary age. What must change are not just our weapons systems but the way we think about security. For, taken together, these revolutions represent the third dimension on the global chess board, a dimension increasingly occupied by stateless nations such as al Qaeda.

This is the challenge we must consider. What does security mean when it no longer means the one-dimensional containment of communism? Does it mean more than the prevention of further terrorist attacks, and, if so, is a "war on terrorism" a sufficient security strategy for this new age? Are you feeling secure, for example, if you have just lost your job? Probably not. Are you feeling secure if your community has just been devastated by its major employer moving off-shore? Probably not. Are you feeling secure if you have just discovered that your children are poisoned by local industrial pollutants? Certainly not. Are you secure if you suspect that your city or state or nation is not prepared for a hurricane or other natural disaster? Of course not. Are you feeling secure when you discover that your teenage son is joining the army to fight for Persian Gulf oil so that your wealthy neighbor can drive his Humvee? Perhaps you had not thought of the trade-off that way. And, of course, you are suddenly highly insecure due to your city being one of several urban centers just put on red alert for probable biological attack by terrorists.

Terrorism is the new substitute for communism. But elimination of terrorism would not provide the cloak of security that most people desire and deserve. The multiple revolutions of the early twenty-first century are compounding insecurity. Yet most political figures are stuck in the one-dimensional twentieth-century world of "national security" sought solely through military preparedness and action, through hammering out a shield. Instead, they should look upon security as the foremost entitlement program of liberal democracies, the new basis for a compact among the people, the nation, and their government, the state.

Shortcomings of the Two-Dimensional Approach in the New Century

National security is being too narrowly defined by the terrorist threat, and the means for achieving it are being too narrowly confined to increased military spending and preemptive warfare. Both propositions must be challenged. National security now has a dramatic new dimension and, while military means are certainly critical to its achievement, a much wider range of policies, beyond unilateral invasion, as in Iraq, are now required.

The limited and often counterproductive nature of a strategy of preemptive war, a strategy that is all shield and an aggressive one at that, means that it falls far short of a grand strategy for the United States. The idea of preemptive attack did not originate with the current administration. The right to defend oneself, to strike first before being struck, has deep roots in English common law and has long been applied to the rights of nations as well. To prevent preemption from becoming a mistake or an alibi, however, a firm legal standard for both individuals and nations has to be met before an attack can be launched: To justify preemptive action, a threat must be *immediate* and *unavoidable*. This standard requires sufficiently reliable information to warrant first action. If the intelligence is wrong, the preemptive attack is unjustified.

If the invasion of Iraq, a preemptive war, simply replaces a secular dictatorship with a theocracy, and if it stimulates increased terrorism against America and the West, then the dominant preemptive idea of our national security strategy has proved both mistaken and counterproductive. If preemptive warfare only has isolated applicability, it fails as a national security strategy, and then the prevailing understanding of security and the range of threats to it are called into dispute. If our true purpose was to establish an American imperium in the Middle East, one based politically and militarily in Iraq, it was never fully disclosed to the American people, and its effect would be to change the very character of the United States from that of republic to that of empire.

Following a prolonged American occupation of Iraq, the death of Yasser Arafat, the assassination of Rafik Harriri in Lebanon, and other events, discussion turned to whether deposing Saddam Hussein has actually led to a revolution in greater Middle Eastern political affairs and thus a vindication of the unprovoked invasion of Iraq. Though the democratization of the region would be a blessing, especially if it is liberal democratization, it is much too soon to claim victory. Even if forms of democracy do begin to emerge in the region, however, two unpleasant facts remain. The scheme to remake the Middle East was never presented as such to the American people openly and honestly, and the manner in which the plan was carried out was an act of empire, however benign, and therefore was a violation of America's character as a republic.

Political nature abhors a vacuum and, between August 1991 and September 2001, a vacuum in national security strategy, brought on by a lack of appreciation for the multiple international revolutions and the need for a new understanding of the nature of security, produced a flawed and potentially dangerous policy requiring a better alternative.

This is by no means to suggest that terrorism is not a threat or that this threat must not be dealt with. To those who disputed the logic of the Iraq war, its supporters were heard to say: "So, you're in favor of doing nothing." Wrong, and wrong again. Those, al Qaeda or otherwise, determined to kill Americans and attack our legitimate interests must be dealt with summarily and harshly by military and paramilitary means, an objective as yet not achieved. Containment of those, like Saddam Hussein, who might potentially provide support for terrorists is both justified and, based on what we now know, effective. Containment and coercive international inspections worked in Iraq, and they will work elsewhere.

But terrorism is a method, not an ideology or even a doctrine. And it is not even a new method. As the military historian Michael Howard has written: "[T]error is only a tool of strategy, not an entity that itself can be fought."[2] A variety of activities to terrorize in-

2. Michael Howard, *The Invention of Peace and the Reinvention of War* (London: Profile, 2001), p. 117.

dividuals and nations, including saturation bombing of cities, has been known throughout human history. While we focus on the terrorists' method, weapons of mass destruction are proliferating and will continue to do so. States are failing and will increasingly do so. Epidemics of AIDS, malaria, and other diseases are spreading in Africa and elsewhere. Climate change is a danger increasingly recognized by all but a fact-denying few. Demand for fossil fuels is outrunning their supply. Globalized trade and information technologies are widening the gap between the haves and the have-nots.

None of these threats to security can be overcome by preemptive warfare. War on terrorism is a necessary but not sufficient objective for America's national security policy, and preemptive invasion is too narrow a method for achieving genuine security.

What is strikingly obvious when security is understood from a larger, multidimensional viewpoint is the limited role that the military plays in achieving it. The largest and most powerful military in the world, now possessed by the United States, cannot create jobs. It does not educate people. It cannot persuade employers not to outsource production. It cannot stabilize the dollar. It cannot and should not enforce our domestic laws and provide public safety. National legislation and policy prevent our regular military forces from enforcing the laws of the United States and even from protecting our borders from encroachment by illegal immigrants.

Military power cannot intimidate us into having confidence in our government. In totalitarian states, dictators try to use armies to achieve all these objectives. In democracies, the army's role is to fight wars to protect our legitimate interests abroad and to defend our shores from attack. Our superior military establishment can provide a shield against terrorism and foreign attack, but it cannot provide a cloak that protects the overall well-being of our citizens. Therefore, as tempting as it may be, to put all our security eggs in the military basket in a revolutionary world is to badly misunderstand both what security means and how we may achieve it in this new age.

An illustration might help. Suppose a family has learned that its neighbor has been robbed. This family, being American, first buys a gun. Then, it seeks more police patrols in the neighborhood. Then, as fear rises, it places double and triple locks on all the doors and windows. Then, all family members take extensive training in the martial arts. Dobermans and rottweilers are brought on board. Expenses mount as ever-greater security is sought. Soon, the roof, needing repair, begins to leak. The furnace's pipes clog, and it blows up. The plumbing in the house deteriorates. Outdoor paint peels and flakes. The kids become ill from lack of outdoor exercise, but the health insurance has lapsed. False reports that someone in the neighborhood is the burglar causes this family to break into the neighbor's house, but no weapons or loot are found. Now our family is increasingly barred from community activities. Barricaded in its deteriorating house, our family has never felt more insecure.

Instead of this self-defeating, insecurity-creating approach, we must first think about what security means as the global neighborhood comes ever closer together. The military power of the United States and the North Atlantic Treaty Organization contained the Soviet Union and, combined with our productive economic systems, ultimately caused it to collapse. We triumphed on the traditional, two-dimensional chess board. Therefore, that same combination of collective security and expanded economic inclusion, increasingly important in the integrated, three-dimensional world, must be used against other new threats, such as the proliferation of weapons of mass destruction.

Military and paramilitary power is central to the defeat of terrorism. But the swamp of despair and hopelessness in which terrorists live and recruit cannot be dried up by the largest military force in the world. Our national house cannot be made safe simply by buying more guns and becoming neighborhood vigilantes. And in a world where man-made cataclysms such as 9/11 compete for attention and resources with natural disasters such as Hurricane Katrina, hard choices will have to be made. What is more important, rebuilding New Orleans or rebuilding Baghdad?

Security's New Dimensions

We must think about security, personal and national, more comprehensively than we did during the Cold War. Security now must mean, at the very least, security of livelihood, security of the community, security of the environment, security of energy supplies, and security from terrorist or other attacks. What makes a person secure? Sufficient income to provide a decent standard of living for oneself and one's family. A stable and safe community. Opportunities for advancement based on education and self-improvement. Affordable health care. A clean environment. A sound currency and stable economy. Secure borders. Public safety created by the internal and external control of crime and by thorough preparation for response to natural disasters. And confidence in our government.

The narrow definition of security is the prevention of physical harm by creating a protective shield. The broader definition of security includes the opportunity for a stable livelihood, the chance to be productive, the comfort of community in a healthy environment, and confidence in the integrity of government—all representing a cloak of protection. Genuine security requires a cloak of economic security, environmental security, health security, energy security, educational security, and government security.

To a degree, the difference in these definitions flows from a difference in outlooks on life. If one believes that life is dangerous, that each of us is pretty much alone, that each must make his own way, that our moral duty is to ourselves alone, and that government's job is to protect us and otherwise leave us alone, then the leaner definition of security as a shield will probably suffice.

THE SHIELD AND THE CLOAK

If, however, one senses that we are all members of a community, that we have a responsibility to look out for each other, that we are all in this together, and that our moral duty is to help to create a general sense of well-being, then one is necessarily drawn to the richer definition of security as a cloak and collective obligation. From the difference in these philosophical dispositions flows political parties and, ultimately, national policies.

Put simply, if security is understood broadly, it will require a much more comprehensive and multidimensional approach to achieving it than a simplistic war on terrorism—and a preemptive war at that.

At this moment, our country continues to pursue a shield definition of security, one that seeks its achievement in the use of military force and preemptive invasion, one whose attempt to keep an integrated world from our doorsteps will prove increasingly futile. Those in favor of these policies argue that they are necessary to bring our values to—some might say, impose our values on—different cultures, in this case, Arab cultures and Islamic societies. Only history can tell us whether they are right. It is, at the very least, a risky way to seek security.

There is a very great difference between imposing values and offering values, between the selective crushing of opposition as a lesson for others and fostering peaceful democratic oppositions, and between an imperial enterprise and a broad-based support for liberal democratic republics.

In the second half of the twentieth century, the United States successfully convinced the rest of the democratic world, much of which was still recovering with our help from World War II, to adopt our world view: opposition to communism. If we now seek to pursue the same policy of imposing a Manichaean world view of good and evil on the much more complex world of the twenty-first century, we will fail. Too many people simply do not see this new revo-

lutionary world in the simple terms that those now in power in
America do.

Our Current Approach and Its Limits

The current administration has two large ideas. One is war on terrorism. The other is the "expansion of freedom in all the world."[3]
There are a number of circumstances where the compatibility of these
goals may be tested. Russia, China, and Saudi Arabia are all under
attack by terrorists. All three are authoritarian states. Does not a war
on terrorism oblige us to side with their governments in destroying
the terrorists in their midst, including the Chechnyans seeking liberty from Russia? On the other hand, if we support the Chechnyans,
as President Bush seemed to be doing before 9/11, or the separatists
in western China in their desire for liberty, are we not undercutting
the war on terrorism?

In other parts of the world, factions are using methods of terrorism in what most claim to be their struggle for liberty from repressive regimes. Does not our support for liberty require us to stand
up for them? There are times and places where one large idea might
have to give way to the other, where eliminating terrorism is in conflict with spreading democracy.

To compound the contradiction, and while crusading for liberty, the United States has now decided to continue down the path
left over from the Cold War and to create a security shield by seeking a kind of empire in the greater Middle East. We will not avoid
the well-known pitfalls that the course of empire contains until a
more comprehensive national security strategy based on both shield
and cloak is adopted. It is the task of those of us committed to this
cause to discover, clear, and place signposts along this new path if

---

3. President George W. Bush, Second Inaugural Address, January 20, 2005.

we are to offer our fellow countrymen and women hope for a genuine security in this new age that combines shield and cloak for the commons.

The Security of the Commons as an Alternative

In the ancient republics of Greece and Rome, from which America's founders drew so many of their ideals and much of their understanding, security was a common good, the product of a shared concern for the commons. The city-state republics of 500 B.C. and the early American republic of the late eighteenth century shared the notion that either all would be secure, or each would go his own way and none would be truly secure. In both those eras, security was seen as collective not individualistic, a shared concern and a feature of the commons which all held together.

Today, this notion of the commons, and the security of the commons, holds a central truth for fashioning a new security policy for a new and remarkably different century. The ideal of the security of the commons, combining cloak and shield, will form the central organizing principle of this search.

A Student of Security

I

There is no guarantee that long years of participation in national security affairs necessarily provide lessons learned. Any number of instances could be cited of well-known political figures, of the Right and the Left, who entered the security debate with fixed ideas and, decades later, retired untroubled by the facts or unaffected by any original thought. To provide any creative contribution to a redefinition of security in the new century, then, requires at least a modest demonstration of lessons learned from a lifetime of studying the military, defense, and national security.

In my case, the lessons learned occurred very much in the context of the traditional military approach to national security. These were the heart of the Cold War years, some much colder than others. In the decade and a half since the Cold War's abrupt end, I've given much thought to the application of these lessons to the revolutionary new age sketched in the previous chapter. I've tried to be sufficiently philosophical in summarizing the lessons learned in the former two-dimensional world so that they have applicability in the new three-dimensional security world.

*Concern for security does not require support for
every war, nor does opposition to one war assume
opposition to a necessary military shield. Democratic
citizens must more thoughtfully decide which wars
they wish to fight, before the wars begin.*

After handing out leaflets for John Kennedy in 1960 and spending the spring of 1968 campaigning for Robert Kennedy, my most
intense political experience was working for George McGovern
throughout 1971 and 1972. That presidential campaign was principally characterized by its opposition to the United States' entangle-
ment in the briar patch of Vietnam and Southeast Asia.

Just two years later, in the Watergate political upheaval, I was
elected to the U.S. Senate and immediately requested membership
on its Armed Services Committee. The Senate Armed Services Committee, like its counterpart in the House of Representatives, authorizes the budget of the Department of Defense every year. This is
done on a line-item basis, that is to say, each category of plane, ship,
tank, torpedo, rifle, grenade, barrack, base, and biscuit is considered
one at a time according to its qualities, quantities, and costs. Further, the committee reviews arms control treaties, considers troop
and fleet deployments, authorizes the opening and closing of foreign
military bases, approves senior officer promotions, reviews troop
combat readiness, assesses recruitment schedules, evaluates military
service academies and schools, and looks after the care and feeding
of military personnel.

Virtually everything having to do with the U.S. armed services
passes under the eye and receives the approval of the congressional
military committees. No senator can know everything (despite a few
who occasionally behave otherwise), not even everything about the
military. Specialization is required and, in my case, it became strategic (nuclear) force structures and arms control, military construction (as chair of that subcommittee), and military reform. The

military reform movement was created by those frustrated by conventional military thinking, bureaucracy, pork-barrel politics driven by the military-industrial complex, and the lessons of Vietnam.

Service on the Armed Services Committee provided a powerful, even unique, perspective on military affairs, the use of force, and defense of the nation. I did not start as a dove, and I did not end up as a hawk. This despite an almost demented insistence by political commentators that we must be one or the other.

Sometimes, war becomes necessary. Sometimes, it is pure folly. Always, it is a terrible waste of lives. Like it or not, in past times a saber rattle might deter those who had in mind to attack us. At least that was true before the age of suicidal terrorism, when war seemed to have a strange logic and reason of its own.

Though I was one of tens of millions of Americans who came to oppose the U.S. war in Vietnam, in my case because I believed the Vietnamese insurgency to be motivated more by nationalism than by communist ideology, I fully understood the need for a strong defense to protect America from any who might genuinely threaten our security. This separated me, at least in part, from those who opposed the Vietnam War simply because they opposed war and the use of military force in general. Then and now, the question is not whether military forces are necessary for national security but rather what *kind* of military forces are most effective when needed.

To question strategies, force structures, and military doctrines is certainly not to oppose the military forces, who have the duty to defend one's country, who know war best, and who often find it least attractive. Some knowledge of military matters is the duty of all citizens.

Moving so quickly and dramatically from war critic in the McGovern campaign days to Senate Armed Services Committee member might seem an enigma. For many in the anti–Vietnam War movement, the U.S. military was the enemy. This was a mistake of huge proportions. Too many on the Left had a simplistic assumption, monumentally wrong, that the military desires war. In democracies at least, that is almost always wrong. One might recall General Robert E. Lee's famous observation that it was a good thing war was so terrible, otherwise it would be too appealing.

The tragedy of killing, of organized effort to slaughter as many of the enemy as efficiently and quickly as possible, can be fulfilling only to the sadistic. And the parody of the military as a home for sadists is nothing more than that. Every civilized military establishment tries to identify the sadist and keep weapons out of his hands. The vast majority of men and women in military service, especially those who make that service a career and even more especially those who have experienced combat, resort to killing only as a last resort and only under civilian command. In an irony echoed thirty-two years later, George McGovern, a veteran of twenty-nine hazardous combat bombing missions, was defeated by a man who never saw conflict.

Beginning with Sun Tzu, all military strategists emphasize that, in winning wars, encirclement, severing supply routes, and breaking the enemy's will to fight are much more effective than direct and bloody assault. If you cause your enemy to lose his will to fight, you win the war. Even in the most progressive democracies, too often the noncombatant, the civilian political leader who has never tasted combat, is the one most willing to commit troops, to order direct assaults on enemy fortifications, to bomb urban targets, to send eighteen-year-old marines into Vietnamese tunnels with .45-caliber pistols and flashlights, or to order house-to-house, door-to-door combat in Falluja. There is something unseemly in this.

Not only should those civilians who savor war be prepared to commit their own sons and daughters to combat, it would be well if they had some firsthand experience of war themselves. At least some members of Congress who supported war in Vietnam were veterans of World War II. Very few of the senior policy makers in the George W. Bush administration and very few members of Congress of both parties who were eager for war in Iraq had ever experienced shots fired in anger.

Concern for the military does not require automatic support for every weapon. Ways of military thinking must always be subject to change. And those who vote for the money should be held accountable for their decisions.

In 1980–1981, I helped to create the military reform caucus in the Congress. This caucus came eventually to be composed of almost one hundred members of the House and Senate, from both political parties. In large part because of polarized clashes over the Vietnam War, liberals and conservatives disagreed on weapons systems, troop deployments, and almost everything having to do with the military. Liberals wanted less; conservatives wanted more. It was a stale, counterproductive, largely useless debate leading nowhere.

Very soon after joining the Armed Services Committee, I tired of this rancor and sought a more thoughtful and productive approach beyond the partisanship and ideology. Through my staff assistant William Lind, I discovered a retired air force colonel named John Boyd and a handful of reformers, including Chuck Spinney and others. They let me sit in on some of their regular meetings, and I discovered an entirely new approach to thinking about the military.

In a word, military reform argues that military thinkers, both civilian and military, learn lessons and fight wars by looking backward; they resist change, form rigid bureaucracies that perpetuate the status quo, are subject to an elaborate military-industrial lobbying system, and are too often driven by ideology, not strategic thinking. Military reform's priorities are people, strategies, and weapons, in that order.

Most military debate has these priorities reversed with very little attention paid to strategy and not a lot to people. People win wars; weapons don't win wars, we argued. You need unit cohesion and the promotion of officers with battlefield imagination and command skills. Then you must have your strategies, tactics, and doctrines right or even the best people will fail. Once again, maneuver warfare—breaking the enemy's will to fight—is more effective than attrition warfare, which involves killing more of the enemy's troops than he kills of yours. And it is not until you have the right personnel policies and strategies, tactics, and doctrines that you decide what weapons you need. This reform thinking process inevitably requires procurement of very different kinds of weapons than conventional thinking produces. More on this later.

Like political campaigns, wars are notorious for being fought using the last war as a model. By nature, military institutions are conservative, that is, they resist change until change becomes absolutely necessary. That is why, even for a dominant power such as the United States, the early stages of war are often costly. Civilian and military leaders think they can simply apply the lessons learned in the last war. Vietnam was not like Korea, and Korea was not like World War II. In World War II, we and our allies were out to conquer, occupy, and democratize Germany and Japan. In Korea, we were trying to drive the North Koreans, and eventually the Chinese, back above the thirty-eighth parallel. In Vietnam, we were trying to keep the Viet Cong from infiltrating and overthrowing the South Vietnamese government.

Iraq is like World War II—*except* in Iraq the war was easy and the occupation hard. There are few insurgencies that are defeated by regular military forces, however powerful, and in Iraq we badly underestimated the ferocity, treachery, and persistence of the insurgency. As we could have learned from the French in Vietnam and didn't, we could have learned from the British in Iraq and didn't.

Secrets are useful and important only if they are true.
But too many secrets are both unimportant and untrue.

In military affairs, the importance of accurate intelligence collection and analysis becomes apparent almost immediately. This was particularly true in my case. Within three weeks of entering the Senate and joining the Armed Services Committee, I was appointed a member of the Senate select committee to investigate the intelligence activities of the U.S. government.

Since its creation in 1947, the Central Intelligence Agency and a burgeoning network of other intelligence agencies had operated without constitutionally required congressional oversight. This massive exception to the mandate of the Constitution was justified on the very simple grounds that duly elected members of the Senate and House could not be trusted to keep secrets. So the less they knew, the better. This worked until the mid-1970s, when reports of serious abuses of power, some known to various administrations and some not, began to surface.

Though a considerable number of senators were either skeptical or outright opposed to investigation, a select committee was created to look into these reports. Joining ten senior senators representing both political parties, I was this committee's youngest and newest member. Throughout 1975 and 1976, we heard secret testimony from the Federal Bureau of Investigation, the CIA, and other officials and heard testimony from both famous Cabinet officers and infamous Mafia dons.

In sum, our committee and thus the nation discovered that there are a great number of secrets in the world, not all of which happen to be true. We also learned the difficulties that a democracy based upon transparency and accountability faces when it tries to carry out far-flung covert operations in the back alleys of the world and resorts to highly undemocratic and unprincipled actions to do so.

*In the long run, there are no secrets, so politicians
should not give a spy a job without assuming
responsibility for oversight.*

The Church committee, as it came to be called after its chair, the
late Senator Frank Church, uncovered plots to assassinate foreign
leaders, overthrow governments, and experiment with drugs, as well
as a bewildering variety of bizarre and not-so-bizarre initiatives undertaken by the intelligence community. The central question was: Who
ordered all of this? In some cases, projects were undertaken by intelligence officials assuming the existence of tacit authority. In many
cases, intelligence agencies were operating under direct orders from
presidents or their advisors.

These were often the worst cases, and if they were disclosed the
intelligence agency involved, usually the CIA, accepted responsibility because the president had to have "plausible deniability" to avoid
political repercussion or embarrassment. For a young, idealistic
American, albeit a senator, it was a harsh education in the dangers
of the politics of expediency. What was perhaps most harsh was the
realization of the ease with which presidents and those around them
could cast principles aside, usually under the convenient and all-
purpose guise of the "national interest."

Tasked during the Eisenhower-Kennedy years with "getting rid
of" Fidel Castro, the CIA set out to seek assistance. Castro and the
United States quickly turned against each other, and access to Cuba
was a problem. Who knew Cuba, and particularly Havana, better
than the Mafia, for the Mafia had pretty much run things there, in
the form of gambling casinos, hotels, nightclubs, and prostitution,
in the Batista (pre-Castro) era. Our committee was told that the CIA
turned, in the early 1960s, to three notorious Mafia figures, Sam
Giancana, Johnny Roselli, and Santo Trafficante, for guidance. The
plots concocted by the CIA-Mafia combine came to naught, though
quite ironically a poison pen was transferred to a putative Castro

assassin in Paris on November 22, 1963, the day John Kennedy was killed.

These and other episodes offer caution about the limits placed on American power less by public disclosure and more by our principles—who we are and what we claim to stand for. To me, there seemed to be a direct correlation between activities requiring departure from America's principles and eventual doom. The intelligence services are fond of saying, and rightly so, that successes cannot be discussed and therefore yield no credits, but failures are always disclosed and held up to ridicule.

There is a good deal of truth to this. Nevertheless, future generations of American political leaders would be well advised to consult our record of covert operations over the past several decades before placing expediency above principle and casually ordering the CIA or any other organization to undertake an operation that clearly violates our nation's principles and pronounced beliefs. Our record in this regard is neither effective nor admirable.

A footnote to the Cuban CIA-Mafia episode has gone largely unrecognized. After testifying before our committee twice in secret, Johnny Roselli was brutally murdered and sunk in a barrel off the beaches of Miami. Sam Giancana was murdered in the basement kitchen of his own Chicago house by six bullets in the throat before he could testify. Neither crime has been solved.

*Politicians must be held accountable if things
go badly. Where U.S. national honor is at stake,
we let most of them off too easily.*

Up to this point, the mid-1970s, the operating principle in the U.S. covert world was plausible deniability. This was a term of art providing cover for the president of the United States. Very few major covert intelligence operations took place before or after this period without the president's knowledge, and they almost always took place with his authorization. These included the overthrow of foreign governments, including Iraq and the Dominican Republic, U-2 spy plane missions over the Soviet Union, the Bay of Pigs invasion, and a bewildering variety of greater and lesser covert activities. Curiously, the Church committee never was able to establish definitely that either Dwight Eisenhower or John Kennedy authorized the assassination of Fidel Castro, among others.

In every case, however, when things went badly, the president in power was supposed to be able to deny knowledge of the operation. Someone had to be held accountable when the story broke, and it was in almost every case the Central Intelligence Agency. Thus, when many of these extraconstitutional projects surfaced during our deliberations, Senator Church himself labeled the CIA a "rogue elephant."

I concluded otherwise. The CIA clearly did what political leaders of the day told it to do. But part of plausible deniability was to leave the means of achieving the covert objective to the intelligence operatives, which further permitted seemingly stunned presidents later to say, "They did *what*? Why would they have done such a thing?"—and not be totally disingenuous. The theory seemed to be that it was better for a president to seem uninformed than to seem culpable. Commentators of the Right later proclaimed that the Church committee had weakened the CIA. This was and is utter nonsense. In our committee's final recommendations, we insisted that future large-scale covert operations be authorized in writing by the president. This had the salutary effect of protecting the CIA from charges of rogue elephantism (if not elephantiasis) and gave a number of future presidents some pause before signing a piece of paper, called a "finding," that authorized the operation.

Take, for example, the Iran-Contra affair in the mid-1980s. The Reagan administration was conducting covert warfare against rebel insurgents in Central America. President Ronald Reagan was later famously to argue that these local insurgents had to be stopped where they were or they would soon be flooding northward across the Rio Grande, a dramatic fiction that he may actually have believed. Predictably, at least to those of us who had explored this treacherous territory a decade before, things began to get out of hand; Congress demanded to know what was going on before it would provide further funds; and the cowboys in the White House undertook to subvert the U.S. Constitution by selling arms to the Iranians and using the proceeds, in contravention of the laws of the United States and the will of Congress, to finance the covert operations in Central America. (Never mind that we were, at this time, also providing support to Saddam Hussein in Iraq's war against Iran.) Cakes in the shape of Bibles got involved and, like all such undertakings, constitutional tragedy turned into espionage farce. Though he was to deny under oath recollection of signing a finding authorizing this escapade, the befuddled president had in fact done so.

What suffered from this opera was not the CIA but plausible deniability. After the convenience of that fig leaf was removed, there have been substantially fewer covert operations, at least unless real national security was at stake and the public would ratify action, though Reagan policy makers convicted of felonious perjury before Congress in connection with Iran-Contra have been restored to positions of power in the George W. Bush administration.

Talk is not worthless simply because it is cheap,
and it is much less costly than spilling blood.

Even while conducting wide-ranging espionage and covert operations against each other, with various fits and starts and occasional diplomatic interruptions, the United States and the Soviet Union explored arms-control negotiations from the relatively early days of the nuclear arms race. Mostly, these negotiations concerned strategic missiles and warheads, *strategic* in this sense loosely used to cover long-range weapons sufficiently powerful as to disable a nation and its ability to wage war (as opposed to tactical, battlefield, or war-fighting weapons). Being the ultimate weapons, those whose use was unimaginable and from whose use recovery was difficult to conceive, they tended to attract one's attention.

There were those in and out of Congress sufficiently traumatized by the very existence of these weapons that they would advocate one or more forms of unilateral arms reduction. At the other extreme were those whose distrust of the Russians was so elemental that they believed that no limitation treaties would be honored and therefore that the enterprise of negotiations was useless at best or folly at worst.

Most of us fell in between, in my case very much on the negotiations side. By the mid-1970s and certainly throughout the 1980s, the United States had more than sufficient overhead satellite capability to monitor Soviet missile tests (more often unsuccessful than successful), track missile deployments, observe prelaunch activities at missile sites, monitor troop movements, and keep the Soviet fleet under surveillance, and we possessed a wide variety of other intelligence collection devices that could measure warhead test detonations, listen to military and political communications traffic, and notice if Soviet leaders suddenly went underground. Nothing big was going to happen without us knowing it well enough in advance to take any action necessary to defend ourselves.

Yet negotiations of arms limitation treaties met skepticism from some and outright opposition from those who simply refused to accept the idea of even talking to the Russians. In the late 1970s, to help satisfy congressional critics of the Strategic Arms Limitation Talks (SALT) that U.S. negotiators were not giving away the store and to lay the base for Senate ratification of a prospective treaty, several congressional observers, including me, were appointed to monitor these talks firsthand.

I visited the negotiations in Geneva several times and talked informally with both U.S. and Soviet negotiators. Our delegation in the late 1970s, headed by the superb negotiator and diplomat Ralph Earle, also had as its military representative an officer who was not sympathetic to his own country's bargaining positions and made it clear to visitors such as myself. There was evidence to suggest that his dissent made its way through a Senate staff member to a conservative Washington columnist. It was, in at least a few cases, possible for the Soviets to read about a forthcoming U.S. negotiating position before it was officially tabled in Geneva, with accompanying reasons that it would never be acceptable to conservatives in and outside the Senate.

One can conclude for oneself, as I did then and do now, the degree to which this conduct represented disloyalty to U.S. national security interests. The staff member in question later joined the George W. Bush administration and would, along with the journalist in question, continue to determine, according to their own ideological barometers and not the due constitutional process of government decision making, what was and what was not in the interest of the United States.

Nevertheless, in the 1980s, Ronald Reagan would approve the negotiation of large-scale arms reduction agreements at least as dramatic and sweeping as those of Jimmy Carter and sell it to those of his own conservative persuasion with the simple, and obvious, slogan: Trust but verify. No one was heard to argue to the contrary before, or since. Prompted by the earlier Reagan arms build-up or not, Mikhail Gorbachev would lose his job and the Soviet Union its identity and its empire in part because of Gorbachev's embrace of dramatic arms reductions. This historic fact has to provide some weight to the efficacy of negotiations between great powers.

Pay attention when your enemy says he is giving up,
and prepare for victory. It might just happen.

In large part because I had been the runner-up for the Democratic party's presidential nomination in 1984, and thereafter was leading in the national polls for 1988, I was invited to meet with President

Gorbachev in December 1986. Based on previous meetings with Soviet leaders, what I had expected would be a rather brief, formal exchange of introductions and prepared remarks turned into an almost four-hour discussion of the range of U.S.-Soviet and world issues. This was followed a day later by a wide-ranging, free-flowing exchange of equal length with the Soviet foreign minister, Eduard Schevardnadze (later president of Georgia), who, like Gorbachev, was just ending his first full year in office.

Much transpired during those five days, not least Gorbachev's release of Andrei Sakharov from internal exile at Gorky (interpreted by some at the time as a gesture of substantial personal good will toward his visitor), but most startling was Gorbachev's statements in our discussions that the Cold War was over, that the Soviet Union saw no clear purpose in perpetuating an unnecessary arms race, and that it was, thenceforth, going to pursue its own reconstruction and internal development under the defensive umbrella of the forces it then possessed.

Upon my return to the United States, I gave a number of speeches and held forth privately that the Cold War was now coming to an end. It turned out to be true. Our nation at that time was unprepared for victory. That is to say, the foreign policy experts, including most of those who had been determining U.S. foreign policy throughout the Cold War, could not really bring themselves to think of a post–Cold War world. Being a bellicose nation, it was argued, the Soviet Union would never turn away from aggression of one kind or another. As an iron-clad empire behind an Iron Curtain, the Soviet Union would be around as far into the future as one could see. It was inconceivable that the Soviet system could produce a genuine reform leadership.

Despite Dwight Eisenhower's warning, a military-industrial complex had by this time spread a vast network of roots and branches throughout both houses of Congress, the White House, and all regions of the American economy and, to the degree that it had a central organizing principle, it was that the arms race would go on pretty much forever—and a good thing too because what would happen to all those jobs if it ever ended?

Sometimes, where national security is involved, events favorable to your well-being and tranquility do transpire. If that possibility has not been envisioned, great chances are missed. We simply could not conceive that our side might actually win the Cold War without firing a shot. The Cold War, and the waste of enormous national resources, continued almost five years after my meetings with Mikhail Gorbachev.

As yet another footnote, had I been elected president in 1988, it was my plan to propose terms of sweeping and verifiable nuclear arms reductions to President Gorbachev following the election and to invite him to the presidential inaugural on the condition that he would be prepared to negotiate within the framework of that agenda. I discussed this with him in later years, and he confirmed that he would have been more than willing to do so. At least the Cold War would have been over a good deal sooner, and we could have gone on with the rest of our national lives.

If warned of danger, pay attention. A new dimension may be added to the security chess board.

At the end of his first year in office, 1991, I sent President Bill Clinton a memorandum entitled "Elements of a New Grand Strategy" and urged him to appoint a commission of elders to consider where America was to go following the end of the Cold War and what its purposes in the world of the twenty-first century should be.[1] The idea came from studying the period of 1946–1947, when President

1. An extract of this memorandum to President Clinton is included, as an appendix, in Gary Hart, *The Fourth Power: A Grand Strategy for the United States in the 21st Century* (New York: Oxford University Press, 2004).

Harry Truman had relied on the advice of a collection of ad hoc committees and commissions to answer the same questions at the end of World War II. President Clinton chose not to act on this perhaps overly grandiose idea, that is, until Speaker of the House Newt Gingrich had a similar, but considerably more limited, version of the same idea and introduced a resolution in Congress in 1998 to create a commission to study our future national security doctrines and structures. The two men collaborated, and the U.S. Commission on National Security/21st Century was created in October 1998, and its final report, dated January 31, 2001, went a good distance toward the goal I had originally proposed to President Clinton almost a decade earlier.

An official national commission with the breadth of mandate that our commission was given had not existed since 1947. It was the most comprehensive review of U.S. national security since the end of World War II and the dawn of the Cold War. It took the commission's fourteen members and staff of foreign policy and national security experts almost two and a half years to complete our work. We publicly issued two interim reports, one in September 1999 and one in April 2000, and were required to submit our final report, containing fifty specific recommendations to improve U.S. national security, to the new president, George W. Bush, who unfortunately could not make himself available to receive it and discuss it with us.

Because most of its recommendations have still not been acted upon, and because it will be some time before another effort of this scope to define national security in the twenty-first century comes about, discussion of the commission and its recommendations will be woven throughout this book. In addition to warning of probable terrorist attacks, one of our most important formative decisions was to define U.S. national security broadly to include what I am describing here as both a shield and a cloak.

Our commission's primary and immediate recommendation was to reorganize the national government by creating a new homeland security agency. This recommendation was motivated by the overwhelming conclusion we had reached as early as the fall of 1999 (almost exactly two years before 9/11) that America would be attacked by terrorists using weapons of mass destruction, that "Americans will die on American soil, possibly in large numbers,"[2] and that we were almost totally unprepared. It was impossible to reach that kind of conclusion, while realizing the miserable state of our nation's readiness, without believing with considerable urgency that steps had to be taken at the earliest moment to prevent such attacks and, if prevention were unsuccessful, to be prepared to respond to them.

Unless we form a posse, we will continue to be the High Noon *sheriff. Security in three dimensions requires close cooperation.*

The end of the Cold War saw a new kind of warfare break out. It baffled us. We were accustomed to great national armies mobilizing and meeting in the field of battle in mass formation almost like the knights of old. Men and matériel were exchanged, and one side won and the other side lost. This is understandable, if not also very bloody, warfare. This did not turn out to be the way things happened in Somalia, in Bosnia and Kosovo, in Haiti, in Rwanda, or in a growing number of obscure places most people had never heard of. What is a superpower to do? We did a number of things, all contradictory and none revealing any understanding of the conflicts of the new post–Cold War era.

2. "New World Coming," First Report, U.S. Commission on National Security/21st Century, September 15, 1999.

In Somalia, we intervened, with some international support, to help humanitarian groups to distribute food to starving villagers. Despite our good intentions and the promises of cooperation from tribal warlords, we ran into a buzz saw, one operated by those very warlords. Food was a political lever and who got it and who distributed it very much was part of a messy and chaotic tribal power struggle. Those in the "technicals," pickup trucks with machine guns mounted in the truck bed, could not have cared less for our good will, our good intentions, or, for that matter, our superpower status. What were we going to do to them—launch cruise missiles? And, if so, against what? Pickup trucks? The warlords handcuffed the world's greatest superpower, and so we had no choice but to go after the warlords. We now know the outcome, and it was predetermined. Read and see *Black Hawk Down* if you want to understand the battlefield of the twenty-first century.

We ran into a version of the same thing—low-intensity urban warfare against insurgents—in Falluja several years later and, though "successful," seem to have learned nothing. We destroyed the city of Falluja in order to save it and, subsequently, insurgents reentered the city. Fighting was still going on months and months later. And it will continue to go on after the last American marine dies in Iraq and the last American marine leaves there.

A superpower that cannot learn will not be a superpower for very long.

In Kosovo and Bosnia, we conducted, with international support, a bombing campaign that cost few, if any, American lives. We still will not reveal the death toll on the ground. But Slobodan Milosevic was deposed and now stands trial, and peace has been restored. In Haiti, we intervened unilaterally. Peace is restored for the time being, but the troubled nation's woes continue, and political strife and economic deprivation characterize the country. The United States, the greatest power on earth, did nothing in Rwanda, and more than 800,000 human beings were slaughtered in a tribal bloodbath.

Things might have gone better for the Tutsis had they been fortunate enough to have oil. Likewise, and perhaps for similar reasons, we stand idly by while yet another ethnic slaughter of innocents takes place in Darfur in the Sudan.

There has been no clear pattern to U.S. policy since the end of the Cold War, principally because we have yet to comprehend the rapidly changing world of the new century. In Gulf War I, under U.N. mandate, we built a genuine coalition of the willing and we had fairly broad-based political support throughout the Arab world. In Somalia, we had U.N. sanction and limited multinational support, which eventually helped us to extricate trapped U.S. forces in downtown Mogadishu. In Gulf War II, we cobbled together a makeshift "coalition" which was 95 percent American and a limited number of British in terms of numbers of troops, costs, and casualties.

There are many reasons that no clear pattern or policy has emerged. We are unaccustomed to a world of disintegrating states, tribalism, fundamentalism, terrorism, chaos, and religious and ethnic warfare. We have not worked out the relative responsibilities of the international community in the form of the United Nations and those of the sole superpower, the United States. There is also no international consensus in this new century over when disputes are to be settled internally and when outside force is required.

As a result, three American post–Cold War administrations have played it by ear and, in the process, we have confused ourselves and confounded the rest of the world.

A great deal of the problem revolves around the distinction between peace keeping and peace making. The U.N. Charter grants the world body a peace-keeping role under circumstances approved by the Security Council. By definition, peace keepers are defensive forces, that is to say, they are trained and equipped to preserve a peaceful situation. Defensive forces prevent violations of an existing peace. These kinds of forces are neither trained nor equipped to *make* the peace, that is, to stop violence in a combat zone. The founders of the United Nations, eager to preserve their national sovereignties, did not grant to the United Nations an active peace-making role.

Given the world of the twenty-first century and the United States' uneven role in it so far, the United States should now propose the creation of an international peace-making force under U.N. auspices. (How this might work is discussed more fully in chapter V.) In the twenty-first century, the United States can either continue down the path of ad hoc intervention according to no known criteria, or it can anticipate more crises of the type that have already come to characterize this new age and take steps to organize an international rapid deployment police force.

If preemptive warfare by the United States was justified in Iraq, why is it also not justified by the United Nations in Sudan to save hundreds of thousands of lives in Darfur? We can continue to be the unpredictable sheriff, who chooses when and when not to enforce the law according to whomever happens to be in power at the time and what ideological biases that party may have, or we can assume that trouble is always with us and organize an international posse to protect peace and guarantee public safety.

Tell the American people the truth and, if they lend
their support, it will be long lasting; if they are lied
to, do not assume their support when things go wrong.
This is a lesson our leaders seem never to learn.

Early in my Senate days, I was told a story by a Senate colleague, the late Gaylord Nelson of Wisconsin, that I have remembered often. He had earlier voted against a nominee for a senior Cabinet position whose background and claims of moral uprightness were unsurpassed. When asked to justify his negative vote, Senator Nelson said: "Something will turn up." And it did. Soon thereafter, the Cabinet officer in question was indicted, convicted, and removed from high office. The story is important not as an illustration of Nelson's prescience but as a warning against those who fly false colors.

In the run-up to the Iraq invasion during the summer and fall of 2002, all now recall the claims of stockpiles of weapons of mass destruction ("They are there and we know where they are," promised Vice President Dick Cheney), determination by Saddam Hussein to attack the United States, and close ties between Iraq and al Qaeda. Though merely a concerned citizen with no vote in the matter, like Nelson before me, I disbelieved the whole thing and said, "Something will turn up." Except in this case, nothing turned up.

The only issue for history is whether we waged preventive war unnecessarily based on staggeringly wrong factual mistakes or whether our nation's leaders were guilty of massive mendacity. Having already disclaimed any ability to read minds, especially those of politicians, one is left with circumstantial evidence. Thoreau once described circumstantial evidence as finding a trout in the milk. In the case of the neoconservative war advocates, the trout was in the form of the Project for the New American Century, a title that tells much about its intentions.

Officially formed in the mid-1990s, but with roots traceable to the first Gulf War and George H. W. Bush's decision not to march on Baghdad, the Project for the New American Century advocated the invasion of Iraq and overthrow of Saddam Hussein as a means of providing a U.S. military and political base in the center of the greater Middle East and using that base to impose terms on the Iranians, Syrians, and others in the region, preventing the overthrow of the Saudi royal family, and guaranteeing Persian Gulf oil exports to the world. If democracy of some kind could be imposed on the inhabitants of the region, so much the better.

The founders of this project, to their credit, were open and straightforward about their agenda—at least at that time. In one form or another, this agenda was advocated in speeches, conferences, and published articles. It was proposed as U.S. policy to President Bill Clinton in an open letter in 1998. It became the centerpiece of neoconservative foreign policy for the twenty-first century some years before the terrorist attacks of 9/11.[3]

All of this is unremarkable, except for one fact. Founders and participants in the Project for the New American Century included Richard Cheney, Donald Rumsfeld, Paul Wolfowitz, Richard Perle, Douglas Feith, and a considerable number of others who shared the distinction of becoming senior figures in the administration of George W. Bush in 2001. Thus, they clearly had in mind a unilateral attack on Iraq years before any declaration of war on terrorism.

In what came to be called the "Downing Street memorandum," minutes of a British Cabinet meeting in the spring of 2002 confirmed that the U.S. government had early on secretly decided to invade Iraq and depose Saddam Hussein, and the facts and the intelligence would be made to support that policy. This trout calls into question the motives for the Iraq war and raises the serious question of whether our government told us the truth about its policies and intentions. Was there a bait and switch? Were we told one thing, that we were attacking a government that threatened our security, which in fact we were doing quite another thing, seeking to use the terrorist argument to carry out a scheme of empire?

3. For the Web site and history of the Project for the New American Century, see www.newamericancentury.org. On January 26, 1998, the principals in this project addressed an open letter to President William Clinton that concluded:

> Given the magnitude of the threat, the current policy, which depends for its success upon the steadfastness of our coalition partners and upon the cooperation of Saddam Hussein, is dangerously inadequate. The only acceptable strategy is one that eliminates the possibility that Iraq will be able to use or threaten to use weapons of mass destruction. In the near term, this means a willingness to undertake military action as diplomacy is clearly failing. In the long term, it means removing Saddam Hussein and his regime from power. That now needs to become the aim of American foreign policy.

The American people are usually slow to anger. But if they conclude they have not been told the truth, those responsible should be prepared to alter their policies—or head for the exit. Rightly or wrongly, and I think wrongly, a certain amount of deception has come to be accepted in American politics. But the patience of the American people is not limitless. The limits on its patience are often measured, tragically, in human lives. At the center of deception where Iraq is concerned is the concealment of casualty figures.

Some, myself included, argued in 2002 and up to March 17, 2003, the day of invasion, that the president should answer four questions before war was launched: Who would go with us? How long would we stay? How much would it cost? And what were the casualty estimates?

Despite the government's insistence on a fiction called "coalition forces," except for a small-scale British deployment, this is an American show. Since the unexpected insurgency has proved to be both durable and expanding, there is no plan for departure. In the spring of 2005, senior military officials predicted that U.S. forces would be required in Iraq for another decade or more. The costs are soaring well above $200 billion, for forecasting which a senior Bush economic advisor, Lawrence Lindsey, was fired, with no sign of ending.

And most troublingly, the casualties mount astronomically. There are well over two thousand dead American military personnel, another twelve to fifteen thousand wounded in combat, and a possible ten thousand American noncombat casualties, including a shocking number with psychiatric disabilities. Civilian Iraqi casualties possibly exceed fifty thousand. Total American casualties are now beyond twenty-five thousand. Given our government's reluctance to disclose these facts, most Americans do not know them.

By late 2005, virtually all polls showed that public support for the Iraqi war, as in Vietnam, has been eroding. It will reach a tipping point, probably triggered by one or more mass casualty attacks against American and Iraqi interests, and public support will melt almost visibly. Then Congress, including members from the president's own party, will say "enough," appropriations will be squeezed, and the executive branch will have no choice but to begin the exodus.

Whether this would all have been different if those transposed from the Project for a New American Century to government power had stated clearly and directly that their desire to overthrow Saddam Hussein was separate from the war on terrorism will never be known. On 9/11, Osama bin Laden gave them the outlines of an excuse, with the blanks filled in with fiction, which was necessary to justify a preventive war long before there was anything to prevent. Had the neoconservatives trusted the good judgment and common sense of the American people, there is a good chance that none of this would have happened. This experience does, however, ratify an insight by one of the United States' most distinguished twentieth-century diplomats, George Kennan, who observed, "[I]t never pays for our government to give false impressions to the American public with the view to enlisting its support for short-term purposes, because this always revenges itself later when it becomes necessary to overcome the wrong impressions one has created."

The American military is a living organism,
not a machine, and even the greatest military force
has its limits.

Civilians who live under the shelter provided by their defense forces normally take for granted that an army replenishes itself when depleted, much like some self-repairing machine. Despite the machine-like qualities that military forces seek to project, the armor may be steel but the people are flesh and blood. And even steel shares some qualities with human beings; both can be bent and broken.

War has its costs. Fighting a war depletes military forces. Most obviously, people are killed and wounded. They must be replaced through recruitment or conscription. Weapons are damaged or destroyed. They too must be replaced. Prolonged wars are the most costly. Over time, people and machines wear down. It is called attrition. To sustain a level of combat readiness, military services and their support structures must replenish themselves at least at the rate attrition occurs. Even for a mighty industrial and economic power, this is not always as easy as it might seem.

The process of regeneration while battle goes on is complicated by the ability of creative enemies to invent new ways of destroying men and matériel at a cost to themselves lower than the cost of replenishment is to us. Iraqi insurgents, though by no means unique in the history of warfare, have nevertheless proved especially adept at inventing mayhem and new forms of destruction. Many of their tactics mirror traditional guerrilla warfare, but they have also managed to combine that style of warfare with conventional terrorist tactics and new forms of suicidal terrorism.

Suicidal terrorism is dependent on two presumptions: a never-ending supply of volunteers and a high level of fanaticism. Precious volunteers will probably not be sent out to blow themselves up if it is known that their supply is limited. It is one thing to sign up for a cause and a dramatically different thing to be willing and ready, especially at a young age, to die for it. Iraqi insurgents have proceeded on the basis that they have a virtually unlimited supply of suicide bombers who will enter checkpoints or troop concentrations on foot or driving vehicles constructed as mobile ordinance or ground-based missiles.

The United States was taken totally off guard by this style of warfare, both in its intensity and its duration. Currently, it seems endless. Its effect, especially in the disputed central region of Iraq, is to drive American forces back to the protection of their strong points, bases, and politically sensitive targets. Thus, the mightiest offensive army in history is forced, with some exceptions, into a defensive position. And the coffins keep coming home.

Military forces cannot solve problems that are political in nature. There is no military solution to the organized chaos in Iraq.

Peace will come to Iraq only through political creativity, not continued violence. Perhaps this suggests a final lesson:

Never try to use military means to impose a political settlement unless you are willing to suffer more losses than your enemy.

Having misunderstood the political situation in Iraq, we should not expect the military to solve it. Great military defeats, as in Vietnam, have resulted from political leaders expecting military forces to do their work for them. It has never happened and it will never happen. By lumping Iraqi nationalist insurgents, largely Sunni, with outside jihadists, largely Saudi, under the umbrella of "terrorists," we have confused an already complex conflict and left ourselves little room for political maneuver.

We learned little from the French experience in Vietnam, and we learned nothing from the British experience in Iraq. The British killed an estimated twenty thousand Iraqis during their occupation in the early 1920s. And, having learned nothing from history, we have been doomed in both cases to repeat it. Meanwhile, the coffins out of sight and therefore out of public mind—continue to come home, home to a country unwilling to face reality, unwilling to ask the questions those young lives deserve, and unwilling to recognize its own folly.

It is, of course, possible to learn the wrong lessons from a lifetime of studying security. Lacking the certainty available only to the orthodox elite, it is certainly possible in my case. In this age where certainty, right or wrong, is rewarded with political power ("I don't always agree with him, but I know where he stands"), to confess uncertainty, lack of understanding, confusion, or doubt is to be guilty of something called relativism. To be in doubt when surrounded by those who know no doubt is to be guilty of a lack of moral clarity and moral certainty. Yet there is a line, however indistinct, between moral certitude and fanaticism.

The lessons suggested here, crystallized from thirty years as a student of national security, will seem obvious to most. Our national security requires the most capable, most modern military in the world. It requires constant reform in a constantly changing age and civilian leadership that appreciates its strengths and its limits. Military power is largely useless if intelligence is not accurate. Civilian political leadership must be forthright and honest with the American people and must accept responsibility for misguided wars. Sophisticated diplomacy can often prevent wars and save lives. Even more than in the past, we will need the help of other nations of good will to help guarantee our own safety.

Despite having spent much of a lifetime concerned with America's national security during and after the Cold War, all these lessons have convinced me that we are now in a new and greatly different age, an age in which the security chess board has important added dimensions. And perhaps all the lessons I have learned lead me to conclude that, in the new age of the twenty-first century, even more than the twentieth, *genuine security cannot be achieved by military means alone*. We must have the military shield, but it must be combined with a cloak that protects us from the dangers that the military cannot.

The Transformation of Security

Bread or Freedom, or Bread and Freedom

II

In the "Grand Inquisitor" chapter of *The Brothers Karamazov*, Fyodor Dostoevsky dramatized the choice now faced by two or three billion people. In the famous narrative of the brother Ivan, given a choice by the Cardinal Grand Inquisitor—who may also be the Devil—between bread and freedom, the Captive who is meant to represent Christ remains silent, but "the end of it will be," says the Inquisitor, "that they will bring us their freedom and place it at our feet and say to us: 'Enslave us if you will, but feed us.'"

This is the crux of the security dilemma in the world of the twenty-first century. It is cruel and unrealistic to assume that political freedom necessarily provides the security of life's basic necessities. There are simply too many instances in the world where it does not. This is not an argument for authoritarian politics. It is an argument for understanding security as something greater than political freedom. It is an argument for defining security and freedom broadly enough to encompass the cloak of livelihood. For if security does not encompass livelihood, those set free by an American crusade can quickly find themselves surrendering that freedom for the bread required to survive. Then, faced with a new authoritarian regime providing bread in exchange for freedom, the United States will, yet again, be tempted to reach for its pistol.

Let's consider in more detail how twenty-first-century security has been transformed into the multidimensional goal it now represents and how those dimensions reveal themselves on the global commons.

The Cold War and the Military Shield

Two world wars offered the proposition that security must be achieved militarily. The Cold War that followed supported this proposition by the success of the encircling military forces that contained communism within its Soviet bloc and prevented it from expanding. One has only to reflect on the Cold War era to appreciate how much more complicated the whole notion of security, particularly national security, has become.

The central organizing principle of the containment of communism was essentially one dimensional. It focused the deterrent shield of military power, especially in the form of strategic nuclear weapons, on the Soviet Union and any ambitions it might have to expand its territory by force or hegemonic influence.

Even then, however, nuance crept in. In only a few cases did we side with insurgents waging wars of liberation from late colonial rule. This was seldom done because most of the late colonial powers were on our side in the Cold War. It was difficult to ask for European support in the containment of communism and resist, for example with the French in Indochina, the efforts of European powers to hold onto their empires. We also assumed in almost all cases that local insurgents were agents of communism, and in those cases where we were wrong or where that alignment was secondary, as in Vietnam, we helped to move local insurgents toward the communist camp by our actions in opposition to them.

Therefore, we were mostly opposed to insurgencies and wars of national liberation however much they might promise freedom for their people. In too many cases, we sided with or practically created oligarchs and dictators, like General Augusto Pinochet in Chile in 1973 and later Saddam Hussein in Iraq in 1982, simply because they proclaimed themselves to be anticommunist, suppressed local insurgencies, or battled with fundamentalists. As the Cold War was exhausting itself in the 1980s, we began to face the rise of religious fundamentalism, not communism, in venues such as the Middle East. Though the Muslim mullahs in Iran who overthrew the shah were militantly anticommunist, we feared the possibility that their radical fundamentalism might spread throughout the region and therefore sided with the dictator Saddam Hussein against them.

Our policy of excruciating expediency remained this: The enemy of our enemy is our friend. There were exceptions. John Kennedy's Alliance for Progress in the early 1960s, following mounting popular protests, sought to bring pressure on Latin American oligarchies to adopt land and tax reforms, to share the wealth and the means of livelihood with the poorest and reduce their vulnerability to communist proselytizing.

And now, beyond the Cold War and in the early years of the twenty-first century, military power certainly overthrew the Taliban government in Afghanistan that harbored al Qaeda. But the top al Qaeda leadership and, as it turns out, much of the Taliban infrastructure, is still at large more than three years later. And the default argument for invading Iraq, that it was done to liberate the Iraqi people, leaves the strong impression that America sees military power as the principal instrument for a quasi-imperial crusade to impose democracy.

Whereas in the vast expanses of the globe where life is lived on the margin and where massive numbers of people do not even have a choice between bread provided by a repressive regime and freedom with no guarantee of bread, in the United States and much of the developed democracies the choice is between the sword and the olive branch. According to one point of view, our nation's security is threatened by external forces, such as it was by German imperialism in the 1910s, by Nazi fascism in the 1930s, by Japanese imperialism in the 1940s, and by Soviet communism in the 1950s, and as it is now by terrorism at the dawn of the twenty-first century. We cannot be secure, it is argued, until these forces are confronted and defeated by military power. Another point of view holds that security is achieved through peaceful means, such as diplomacy, negotiating with antagonistic interests in a way that recognizes their legitimate grievances and desires. The first are called realists, hard-liners, or confrontationalists by the second group, and the second are called idealists, soft-liners, or accommodationists by the first group. By and large, both groups have defined security narrowly to mean the reduction or elimination of a physical political and military threat.

In the early twenty-first century, the ground has shifted in complex ways. Those formerly considered hard-liners, now called neoconservatives, have assumed an idealistic mantra that involves America as global liberator, nation builder, and democracy imposer, often in unilateral fashion. And, contrariwise, former idealistic progressive Democrats have become international realists.

These contesting views of international politics and America's role in the world dominate the debate over international affairs. The foreign policy scholar Robert Kagan, in contrasting the difference between the European and the American outlooks on the world in an admittedly overly generalized fashion, has the Europeans "entering a post-historical paradise of peace and relative prosperity, the realization of Immanuel Kant's 'perpetual peace'" while present-day Americans remain "mired in history, exercising power in an anarchic Hobbesian world where international laws and rules are unreliable, and where true security and the defense and promotion of a liberal order still depend on the possession and use of military might." Where major strategic issues are concerned, he famously concludes from this, "Americans are from Mars and Europeans are from Venus."[1]

The greatest danger in reducing Americans to Martians is in believing that the challenges of the twenty-first century lend themselves to solutions based on the use of force and that our dealings with the world should best be conducted through the Department of Defense. This Martian outlook on reality is colorful but simplistically one dimensional and fraught with all the perils of backlash. Simply because we have the world's largest and best army does not mean it is always the only or even the best way to solve problems or achieve security. America's military affluence can become dangerous when overtaken by arrogance.

Military power is still important to the success of security but is less definitive of it, and therefore reducing the Western world to Martians and Venusians becomes more problematic. Living as we are in such a revolutionary age, globalization, information, eroding state sovereignty, and the changing nature of conflict are redefining the human condition and national and international realities. As a consequence of these revolutions, insecurity is rising and the traditional means of guaranteeing it, such as military power and diplomatic influence, are each proving inadequate by themselves to provide a cloak of protection against new turbulences.

The Crusade for Freedom: What Is Freedom?

One evolving point of view that seeks to take account of these revolutions is a variation on the confrontationalist idea. It argues that security in democracies cannot be achieved so long as there is not universal freedom in the world. The second Bush administration now represents this point of view and claims roots in the idealism of

---

1. Robert Kagan, *Of Paradise and Power: America and Europe in the New World Order* (New York: Knopf, 2003), p. 3.

Woodrow Wilson who, famously, wished to make the world "safe for democracy." Having no ideology such as fascism or communism to confront, neoconservatives now confront unfreedom itself. Few could be found in favor of "evil" in the first Bush administration, and fewer still will be found in favor of enslavement now.

But, as always when grand and morally unchallengeable crusades are announced, the devil is in the details. How, exactly, is universal freedom to be achieved? What means are to be used? Are they principally military or will they also include diplomacy, economic development, and political persuasion? Woodrow Wilson, we must remind ourselves, proposed to carry out his democratic mission peacefully, not militarily, and in collaboration with the democratic nations of the world, not unilaterally.[2]

Since the greatest tyrant in the world today is poverty itself, are neoconservative Americans now prepared to fork over the tax dollars required to lift the iron cross of disease, hunger, and poverty from the backs of the enslaved billions in Africa, Latin America, and Asia? If so, why not propose a global Marshall Plan with the goal of eliminating poverty by the mid-twenty-first century? Now we can quickly see that the most important question is this: Who gets to define unfreedom?

The new crusaders undoubtedly have a narrower definition of unfreedom—as they have in the past had a narrower definition of security. The tyranny over which they propose to triumph is political oppression, a very worthy goal indeed. Once free, so the think-

2. "[A]lthough partisans of the Bush administration repeatedly described its rhetoric of democratization and humanitarian intervention after 2001 as Wilsonian, such an attribution is quite wrong in historical terms, for President Woodrow Wilson also believed passionately in the creation of international institutions and in exerting U.S. power and influence through those institutions" (Anatol Lieven, *America Right or Wrong: An Anatomy of American Nationalism* [New York: Oxford University Press, 2004], p. 12).

ing seems to go, the humble fisherman living, if at all, on his daily catch, the dirt-poor farmer without a crop, the village woman walking miles for water each day, the dwellers in the favelas, ghettos, and slums of the world's great cities will all be free to make their own way somehow unencumbered by political oppression. Once "free," presumably they are on their own, in much the same way the poor in America are free to become millionaires. It is up to them. But if this new freedom somehow does not produce better than a dollar a day, it will not be long before another dictator comes along who will guarantee the meager dollar a day, and we will be right back where we started before the grand crusade began.

Perhaps the most dramatic illustration of this fact is represented by postcommunist Russia, which, ironically, was the home of Fyodor Dostoevsky. Communist rule was the greatest source of oppression in the second half of the twentieth century. We spent the entire Cold War period condemning this oppression in the Soviet Union, China, and Eastern Europe. Then, Russia freed itself from authoritarian control in 1991, and the process of democratization began. Very soon, however, free market forces consolidated ownership of the means of production in the hands of a few financial oligarchs who essentially replaced the state but felt no need to provide social services. Having few systems to provide a social safety net, most of the Russian people now find themselves free politically but worse off materially than under the former regime. And they are permitting the consolidation of political power in the hands of President Vladimir Putin who has promised them a restoration of the security of a strong central police force but is reducing the state-sponsored social safety net. They are trading their brief moment of political freedom without even the guarantee of bread.

A more serious approach to the expansion of freedom than that of the Bush second inaugural address will recognize that tyranny, oppression, and dictatorships are almost always bitter fruits of the tree of poverty, want, ignorance, disease, and hopelessness. If we wish to get rid of the fruit, we must begin by eliminating the tree. It does not work the other way around. Thus, if the crusade against unfreedom is defined with a proper understanding of the true nature of oppression, we should all sign up for it. Somehow one suspects this is not what the freedom crusaders have in mind.

Because if freedom is white and unfreedom is black, there is an area of grey and plaid which is neither one nor the other. As difficult as it will be for the freedom crusaders to adopt the broader understanding of unfreedom suggested here, it will be even more difficult for them to deal with a nation ruled by an oligarchy where there are cars aplenty but women are not allowed to drive them, councils of government which only family members may join, no free elections, or free press, or freedom of worship, or freedom of assembly, no parliament representative of the people, no opposition parties, and no dissent. Let's call this country Saudi Arabia for convenience, and let's suppose, as is true, that we depend on this country for massive amounts of oil to fuel our massive vehicles. Because of this dependence, the good will of Saudi Arabia is vital to our own freedom— and our security. Faced with an embarrassment such as this, what is a freedom crusader to do?

Consider a nation in Asia with declared nuclear weapons, announced animosity toward the United States, and a brutal dictator who enslaves his people, starves millions of them, and has an army of a million men within thirty-six miles of the capital of his southern democratic neighbor. Let's call this country North Korea. There is no nation on earth more oppressive and less free. We invaded Iraq, it was later explained after weapons of mass destruction seemed to evaporate into thin air, to eliminate a brutal dictator. No similar call regarding an invasion of North Korea has been heard. How is it being proposed to free the North Korean people?

Let's say there is another country bordering on Afghanistan. It is ruled by a general; it also is, shall we say, less than democratic; it oppresses half its population, who happen to be women; and it is economical with freedom. Let's call it Pakistan. However, since the man responsible for killing three thousand Americans, Osama bin Laden, is reportedly hiding somewhere on the Pakistan-Afghanistan border, we need the cooperation of Pakistan's otherwise repressive army and the good will of its less than democratic government to continue our four-year-old search for bin Laden "dead or alive." In this country, as in Saudi Arabia, we will continue to "encourage" freedom, say the freedom crusaders.

If the commitment to free the world, as applied to places like this, consists simply of promoting and encouraging freedom, then there is little difference between this loudly proclaimed policy of global liberation announced by George W. Bush and the policies of less ebullient previous administrations. President Bush finds himself between the noble idealism of his missionary zeal and the cruel realism of U.S. national interest, including interests such as big cars and cheap oil that are difficult to justify. Given our need to get along with some unfree, undemocratic governments, often in the interest of our own economic life style, we will find ourselves toning down our rhetoric and holding our tongue in the face of societies that do not meet our high standards.

On close analysis, this interpretation of the idealism of Woodrow Wilson begins to look much more like the realism of Henry Kissinger, especially in the new three-dimensional world of the twenty-first century.

We should surely all agree that freedom is prized and that all peoples in the world should be free. We should also agree that a world of freedom would be a much more secure world. The expansion of freedom, then it is agreed, must be part of our effort to achieve security. In fact, the expansion of freedom in the sense argued for here—elimination of enslavement by poverty, disease, ignorance, and hopelessness as well as political oppression—is a major contribution to the redefinition of the nature of security, which is central to my argument.

Security and Freedom

Even so, Americans are not secure, or perhaps not even totally free themselves, so long as there is not a reasonable assurance of livelihood for oneself and one's family, reasonable access to at least minimal health care, reasonable protection from environmental pollution, and achievable independence from unfree oligarchies for energy supplies. Reliance on qualifiers such as "reasonable" represents a stipulation that security is relative, that there is no absolute security even from the threat of terrorism on our home soil. Therefore, the large-scale definition of security that combines shield and cloak is by no means utopian. Absolute security, a nirvana free from all danger, is not achievable. Security has many dimensions and it is also relative. And in a democracy of rights and freedoms, security must be balanced with liberty. Always subject to public debate and discussion, some liberty must be sacrificed—say, for example, in submitting to airport searches—to achieve greater degrees of security.

A more textured definition of security in the twenty-first century includes an understanding that security is not absolute, nor is it utopian, nor is it without cost in terms of liberty. Ironically, while we go about liberating others around the world, we may find reality requiring us to forfeit some freedoms to achieve higher degrees of protection from attack. This is particularly true if we continue to liberate people in the Arab world by preemptive warfare.

Unlike the conflicts of the twentieth century, twenty-first-century insecurities are not ideological; they are transnational and more economic, social, political—and cultural—than military. Consider, for example, the failure of states; the proliferation of destructive technologies; mass migrations from the south to the north; global warming and climate change; AIDS, malaria, and other pandemics; and the rise of religious fundamentalism, tribalism, and ethnic nationalism. Certainly, combating terrorism requires military and paramilitary means, and to a lesser degree those means are sometimes also required to deny weapons of mass destruction to rogue states and nonstate actors.

Even in the latter category, however, the case of Dr. Abdul Q. Khan, head of Pakistan's nuclear program, illustrates the limits of military power. Khan ran a personal nuclear department store specializing in selling nuclear weapons-making technology to all comers with a ready checkbook. All these threats to stability operate against the backdrop of impoverishment already discussed. In this world, as on a tossing ship, what is unstable is also insecure.

A central question to be confronted is whether our own life styles, our habits, our patterns of consumption may not be closely related to our new sense of insecurity.

Crusade for Freedom: Life Style and Hypocrisy

The case of oil is an especially troubling one. We are forced to support the undemocratic Saudi oligarchy because of our need for its oil. This oligarchy is antagonistic to the kind of liberty we have made it our purpose to promote. President Bush has stated that the United States will provide support to opposition and insurgent leaders who support democracy in oligarchic states. Presuming such leaders existed in Saudi Arabia, and few so far have publicly surfaced or remained out of jail, would the United States support them, even covertly, and risk the certain wrath of our single most important oil supplier?

What if a Jeffersonian law professor in Pakistan declared her public commitment to the freedoms contained in the U.S. Constitution, and then her efforts to create a democratic political party were crushed and she were imprisoned? Would we champion her cause and insist on her liberation? What of the Chechnyans whose demand for freedom from Russia seemed to have been espoused by President Bush before 9/11 and ignored since then? Will we smuggle Bibles and money into the People's Republic of China if such acts caused the PRC government to stop purchasing U.S. debt? Will we send an army to overthrow President Robert Mugabe of Zimbabwe, a dictator as cruel to his people as Saddam Hussein ever was?

The answer to all these questions, questions far from hypothetical in nature, is of course "no." Self-interest will trump even the current hard-nosed variation on Wilsonian idealism and inaugural rhetoric every time. But a more complex, yet more straightforward and realistic national security policy which appreciates security's new dimensions, addressing the true causes of twenty-first-century insecurity and providing a cloak with the shield, can actually achieve a much greater degree of security than the strategy of preemptive war and pseudo-idealistic rhetoric.

The more chaotic and unscripted the twenty-first-century world seems, the more important the integrity of our political relationships and their conformity to our proclaimed ideals becomes. Oil may be a good place to start. We've noted the embarrassing contradiction between our dependence on oil controlled by an undemocratic Saudi oligarchy and our announced commitment to freedom and democracy. We have many choices to resolve this contradiction, but two stand out: Either continue dependence on Saudi oil and mute our missionary efforts on behalf of democracy or undertake a national energy independence effort (a "send a man to the moon in a decade" kind of commitment) that would free us from our own sophisticated enslavement by an oligarchy and send notice that we take the promotion of freedom and democracy seriously enough to make some sacrifice in order to be free to promote freedom for the Saudi people.

As a result, we might or might not free the Saudi people, but we most certainly would dramatically increase U.S. national security and quite probably save the lives of future generations of American military personnel otherwise to be lost in future Gulf Wars III, IV, and V, and we would redeem our national honor.

Until recently, a national energy security policy might have included shifting imports from the Persian Gulf to Russia. Now Russia itself is slipping toward oligarchy and oppression, and the promise of Russian democracy is dimming. During the Cold War, it was imperative that U.S. political figures visiting the Soviet Union raise the plight of refuseniks, especially Russian Jews, those seeking the right to emigrate, divided families, and those seeking medical treatment in the West. Soviet leaders tired of the harangues, dismissed them as dictated by American political concerns, and, until the waning days of the Soviet Union, paid little serious heed. Yet today, when the Western voice might be as effectively heard, it has been largely silent.

Liberal political figures such as Vladimir Rhyzhkov, journalists who dissent from official government policy, and independent businesspeople arc jailed, marginalized, or harassed, and innocent Chechnyan civilians are brutalized in the name of counterterrorism, all with little vocal protest from the United States. Making Russia the centerpiece of our freedom crusade could liberate the Russian people, provide a genuinely democratic oil supplier in the service of energy security, contribute geostrategically to U.S. national security by bringing Russia fully into the West, and help us to redeem our national honor.

The United States is politically, and perhaps even morally, handcuffed by its dependence on other nations to finance huge government deficits and the massive debt created by our consumption of more goods and services than we produce. One of those creditor nations is the People's Republic of China, decidedly not a free, democratic society. Yet, because China invests in U.S. government securities and therefore finances both our huge foreign debt and our life style of consumption, we have toned down our insistence on democracy and human rights for the Chinese people. As of the inaugural address of January 20, 2005, it seems that our policy will be publicly and rigorously to support dissident political and press leaders in China who oppose their government. We shall see. A considerable degree of skepticism is called for on this score because of our addiction to debt and consumption. Will we require ourselves to live within our means and turn our backs on Chinese credit in order to be free to promote freedom in China and to redeem our national honor?

As with Saudi Arabia and Russia, the case of China illustrates not only the way that some of our core policies and practices seriously constrain our freedom to promote freedom but, more important, it illustrates the way that they undermine our national security. Oil dependence, the good will of a Russian oligarch, the hunt for bin Laden on Pakistan's border, debt, consumption, and borrowing from China all make us insecure. Therefore, there is a direct and dramatic connection between limits on our ability to promote freedom, the unsupportable addictions we have developed, and our national insecurity.

Preemption and Its Limits

Presently, our national security strategy is to seek cooperation and good will from other nations on matters of common and international concern but to reserve to ourselves the right to invade any nation we believe is preparing to attack us and to have as our national policy the right to maintain military superiority over any other nation or indeed the rest of the world. "To forestall or prevent . . . hostile acts by our adversaries, the United States will, if necessary, act pre-emptively," the National Security Strategy of the United States declares.[3]

This strategy correctly recognizes that the United States has long maintained the preemptive option to counter "a sufficient threat" to its national security, though what constitutes a sufficient threat is purposefully left undefined. Indeed all states, as well as all individuals, reserve the option to take preemptive action against any threat to their safety and survival, but, under early common law and later international law, they can only do so, as already pointed out, if such

3. White House, "The National Security Strategy of the United States of America," September 2002. Available at www.whitehouse.gov.

a threat is immediate and unavoidable. Such a threshold is required by law to prevent first-strike attacks on a contentious neighbor or state based upon a false pretext or long-standing grudge.

The Bush doctrine continues on this theme by saying that "anticipatory action" will be resorted to "even if uncertainty remains as to the time and place of the enemy's attack." This means that a sufficient threat need not be immediate and unavoidable to justify a preemptive attack or invasion, thus substantially lowering the traditional legal standard for preemptive warfare. The alternative given, to "remain idle while dangers gather," is not one espoused by anyone willing to do so publicly.

Dependence on an ancient right to preemptively forestall an imminent attack is based on several conditions. The first is that we can know when an attack is being prepared. The second is that we can distinguish between a theoretically possible attack and an attack that is threatened imminently. If it is the first, as was not the case in Iraq, then a first strike is not preemptive, it is preventive, an entirely different and considerably more dangerous doctrine. In either case, highly reliable intelligence is required to know which states have weapons of mass destruction and the ability to deliver them and which states have those weapons, the means to deliver them, and the *intent* to do so within a reasonably foreseeable time period.

These requirements place a heavy burden on intelligence services to get information and an equally heavy duty to get it right. This also was a critical failure in Iraq which, it turns out, was not only incapable of attacking us immediately, it was also incapable of attacking us any time in the foreseeable future. For some in power, it was sufficient justification to wage preventive war merely to say that it was conceivable that at some time in the distant future Iraq might obtain mass-casualty weapons and the ability to deliver them and then surely, or perhaps just possibly, would do so. But even that highly tenuous doctrine ultimately gave way to the default position that Saddam Hussein was an evil dictator and good riddance.

For those of a more serious frame of mind, however, the issue of intelligence becomes critical. It is difficult to determine whether a nation does or does not have weapons of mass destruction, although it is somewhat easier to determine whether that nation has the means to deliver them. Long-range missiles require elaborate facilities for construction and even more elaborate facilities for testing. As previously indicated, our overhead reconnaissance satellites are absurdly accurate at this kind of detection. These same assets are equally good at detecting any wholesale biological, chemical, or nuclear weapons production. The possible exception is relatively small-scale production of biological weapons which, experts say, can be carried out in discrete, and therefore difficult to detect, laboratories. Those same experts say that upward of twenty nations are working to produce biological weapons capabilities, in addition to the two or three dozen nations that already have them. These numbers seem to suggest that the cat representing biological warfare has probably already escaped the preemptive/preventive bag—unless we intend to invade, serially or simultaneously, two or three dozen nations.

For the traditional common law and international law standard to be met—justifying preemptive warfare on the basis that a threat is immediate and unavoidable—however, intelligence must really be good. It must clearly establish not only the capability to produce and deliver weapons of mass destruction but also the intent to do so. There are only three ways to confirm intent: interception of written or spoken communications, deduction, or mind reading. The Pearl Harbor attack is an illustration of the first. There were a lot of Japanese military communications, coded and clear, leading up to the attack. The U.S. military intelligence services knew something was up, possibly something big, but they could not identify a time or a place. Based upon stated and unstated Japanese intentions in the western Pacific, they deduced it would possibly be an attack aimed at occupying Western oil facilities in the region. These deductions were correct, but only in part.

Six decades later, the United States deduced that Iraq was producing weapons of mass destruction because it had tried to do so in the past, that it was perfecting something like the Scud missile system used ineffectively in Gulf War I, that it was preparing to attack the United States because it had previously attacked Kuwait, that it was supporting al Qaeda because it had provided some support to Hezbollah, that it intended to dominate the greater Middle East, and a variety of related deductive conclusions. All these deductions seem to have followed from an early 2001 deduction (or, perhaps better, an obsession) that Saddam Hussein represented a greater threat to U.S. national security than did Osama bin Laden. If there was concrete intelligence based on communications intercepts or live defectors, not just self-interested exiles, to support these deductions, it has never been made publicly available. All these deductions proved to be as wrong as the deduction that Japan's imperial interests were narrowly confined.

The third category, mind reading, is not as fanciful as it sounds. The intelligence community experimented with this capability literally and figuratively during the Cold War and beyond, literally through telepathy and mental profiling and figuratively through projecting patterns of behavior that operated on the border of deduction. Regardless of the limited faith that most people might be prepared to place in mind reading as the basis for a major military invasion, it does seem to have represented an uncanny attraction to pro–Iraq invasion advocates in 2002 and early 2003 who presumed to know what Saddam Hussein was thinking.

Intelligence accurate enough to encompass the intention of a presumed enemy must also be accompanied by some degree of international support to justify preemption as the centerpiece of a security policy. The likelihood of worldwide scorn should be a brake on unwarranted or unnecessary preemptive attacks. Before a summary invasion, any nation should know that, despite its size and power, if its justification is flawed, it will be considered a renegade in the international community. Without such a political and diplomatic constraint, aggressive nations or those with long-held grievances can simply march across sovereign borders any time they choose in order to settle old scores, penalize an opponent, acquire territory, or secure resources and pay no penalty in the court of world opinion.

Having declared that it would give Saddam Hussein a fair trial and then hang him, the United States now has to find a new case to make before this court. American frontier justice may have been summary and blunt, but it was seldom rendered without some claim of legal right.

In addition to accurate intelligence and a justifiable claim of legal necessity, a twenty-first-century security policy premised on preemption requires consistency or at least the avoidance of arbitrariness. If the United States invades Iraq simply because it is alleged to possess weapons of mass destruction, then it would seem to be required to invade all states with weapons of mass destruction that are not friendly to the United States. This category encompasses a number of states, including most prominently North Korea and Iran. If the United States invades Iraq simply because Iraq once invaded a neighboring state, then the United States would seem to claim the right to do so universally. This category—attacking invaders of other countries would include both North Korea and Iran and also a number of others.

If, however, the United States invades Iraq because it is ruled by a dictator, it claims the right to do so elsewhere in a world with a fair-sized population of dictators. The point becomes obvious. If the United States claims the right of preemption, it is plausible to assume that the reasons given will be applied universally, or else the United States is declaring itself to be an arbitrary power reserving to itself the right to determine when, where, and under what conditions it will invade other countries. This is the definition of a bully at best and a renegade at worst.

It will be argued with some plausibility, however, that the United States is not like other nations, that it is a greater target for terrorism as proved by 9/11, and that it is a superpower with special responsibility to maintain world order. But if this special status gives the United States extraordinary rights, it also places exceptional burdens and responsibilities on the United States to justify its actions and to make sure it is not casual with the facts. By slipping, with some seams showing, from the absolute assurance of the presence of weapons of mass destruction, murderous intent against the United States, and support for al Qaeda, to the *potential* for all these things, and then on to cruel dictatorship, as serial arguments for preemptive warfare against Iraq, the United States weakens its own standards and undermines its own legal, political, and moral justification.

Fourth-Generation Warfare

All this insistence on the accuracy of intelligence, plausible justification in world opinion, and consistency in application neglects a brutal new reality that further undermines traditional arguments for preemptive warfare against other nations as the basis for national security. Since 9/11 particularly, increasing attention has been paid to the fact that warfare is being waged less and less between nation-states and more and more by tribes, clans, gangs, and terrorist organizations, all now called "nonstate actors."

These constitute the third dimension on the twenty-first-century's security chess board. Understanding them and fashioning new shields and spears against them is essential to the security of the commons.

While the United States has handcuffed itself to a vile insurgency in Iraq, it is proving incapable of locating Osama bin Laden, let alone smashing terrorist organizations, drug cartels, and mafias or controlling murderous tribes and warlords, vicious gangs, and violent clans that support and are often interwoven with them. Further, there is a dawning and dreadful recognition that *the enemy may already be within our gates.*

Fourth-generation warfare, a notion usually identified with William Lind, a brilliant military thinker, and a small group of equally creative military officers and reformers, is what we now confront.[4] Lind's group of reformers has not been working alone. Fifteen years ago, an equally brilliant Israeli military historian, Martin van Creveld, produced a prescient book entitled *The Transformation of War* in which he forecast the decline of nation-state wars and the rise of low-intensity urban conflicts involving tribes, clans, and gangs.

Lind's concept of fourth-generation warfare includes but is not limited to terrorism. Terrorism is one of a number of ancient and modern methods used by fourth-generation warriors to achieve their objectives. "Terrorism is merely a technique," Lind writes, "a common one in 20th century warfare in the form of terror bombing by aircraft."[5] To put it differently, today's terrorism is a method of warfare carried out by often suicidal people with no fixed address. The objectives of nonstate terrorists are usually much different from those of traditional warfare waged by nation-states. Fourth-generation warriors seek to punish traditional political and military powers for past behavior or convince them to alter their behavior in the future. Fourth-generation warfare carried out by nonstate actors often has no political objective that can be satisfied by negotiated settlement or diplomacy or even formal surrender.

According to Lind, first-generation warfare featured orderly battles using classic line-and-column tactics, and it characterized the period from the peace of Westphalia in 1648 until the mid-nineteenth century.[6] Mass armies and more rapid-fire weapons began to break down the culture of order, and by World War I it began to be replaced by French-style attrition warfare based on centrally controlled

---

4. See William S. Lind, Keith Nightengale, John F. Schmitt, Joseph W. Sutton, and Gary I. Wilson, "The Changing Face of War: Into the Fourth Generation," *Marine Corps Gazette,* October 1989, pp. 22–26. Lind, Schmitt, and Wilson published a follow-up piece, "Fourth Generation Warfare: Another Look," in the December 1994 *Marine Corps Gazette.*

5. See Lind's regular column series, "On War," which is archived at www.military.com.

6. Lind et al., "The Changing Face of War."

firepower, which sought to preserve some degree of battlefield order and represented second-generation warfare, and by German-style maneuver warfare representing third-generation warfare based on speed and battlefield initiative rather than mass firepower and central control. The two generations met in 1940, and the German blitzkrieg, or lightning war, enabled Germany to defeat France's static defenses in fewer than forty days.

Fourth-generation warfare, continues Lind, has three major characteristics: the loss of the state's monopoly on war; a return to a world of cultures not nation-states ("the clash of civilizations" in Samuel Huntington's phrase); and the arrival of this new warfare on American soil.[7] All this was outlined in the *Marine Corps Gazette* and the army's *Military Review* by Lind and his army and marine colleagues as early as 1989, it is important to note, not after 9/11.[8]

Like the National Security Commission's warning in early 2001, Lind's analysis and predictions "elicited no reaction" from civilian or military authorities. But he was not ignored by everyone. One Internet site, discovered by the Middle East Media Research Institute in February 2002, contained an article entitled "Fourth Generation War" and this statement:

> In 1989, some American military experts predicted a
> fundamental change in the future form of warfare. . . .
> They predicted that the wars of the 21st century would be
> dominated by a kind of warfare they called "the fourth
> generation of wars." . . . This forecast did not arise in a
> vacuum—if only the cowards (among the Muslim clerics)
> knew that fourth-generation wars have already been proven;

7. Lind actually outlined the "clash of civilizations" in a major piece published several years before Huntington's famous *Foreign Affairs* article. See Lind, "Defending Western Culture," *Foreign Policy,* Fall 1991, p. 40.

8. "The Changing Face of War" was published simultaneously by the *Marine Corps Gazette* and *Military Review,* October 1989.

> in many instances, *nation-states have been defeated by stateless nations. . . .* The time has come for the Islamic movements facing a general crusader offensive to internalize the rules of fourth-generation warfare. [emphasis added]

The Internet magazine site was called *Al-Ansar: For the Struggle against the Crusader War* and the author was one Abu 'Ubeid Al-Qurashi. The Web site belonged to al Qaeda.[9]

Of course, five months earlier, fourth-generation warfare, carried out by a stateless nation, a culture, against the world's greatest military power, at least in second-generation warfare terms, paid its deadly visit to the United States. Four years later, the top leaders of the stateless nation of al Qaeda have yet to be apprehended. As William Lind has written, "The eternal nightmare of the military theorist is that only the enemy will pay attention to his work."[10]

The implications of Lind's theory of fourth-generation warfare, who carries it out and against whom it is carried out, are ominous in the extreme for America's future security. This is especially true while the United States continues to employ second-generation warfare against fourth-generation warriors on their own soil.

The central battle of post-invasion, occupied Iraq occurred at the city of Faluja in the fall of 2004, a year and a half after the president declared the mission to conquer Iraq accomplished. The conquest of this insurgent hold-out required heavy aerial bombardment, the late twentieth-century replacement for long-range artillery; produced heavy American and civilian casualties (even estimated figures were never released); and reduced the "liberated" city to rubble and made most of it uninhabitable—and yet weeks and months later, pockets of insurgency remained or were recreated. And it is

9. William S. Lind, "Wars without Countries," *American Conservative*, April 7, 2003, pp. 19–21. See also "Special Dispatch—Jihad and Terrorism Studies," Middle East Media Research Institute (MEMRI), 10 February 2002, no. 344.

10. Lind, "On War," www.military.com.

now believed that most of the insurgents had abandoned the city before the U.S. assault took place. The eminent military historian Michael Howard predicted this outcome: "Tomahawk cruise missiles may command the air, but it is Kalashnikov sub-machine-guns that still rule the ground."[11]

The best that can be said for the Iraqi occupation is that it may, at a very heavy cost, provide valuable lessons for U.S. military forces concerning twenty-first-century fourth-generation warfare. As the enormous waste of World War I led to third-generation warfare, so the enormous waste of Iraq may, sadly, lead to a better understanding of the security threats of the twenty-first century and how to deal with them.[12] But given the persistence of gravity, custom, and tradition, there is no guarantee of it. Perhaps among the captains and colonels in Iraq there will be someone who becomes chair of the Joint Chiefs of Staff or secretary of defense and who will bring true reform to America's strategies, tactics, and doctrines and its military structures. In the meantime, as William Lind says concerning the military occupation of Iraq, "nothing could be more useless in countering Fourth Generation, non-state enemies like al-Qaeda."

Naturally, physical security from violence, especially at home, is central to the new concept of security proposed in this book. Part of the reason that security must be considered anew, however, is because the homeland, post-9/11, has become highly insecure. Though current leaders cling to the hope that war can be kept at a distance, few thoughtful experts believe this can be done, and a large number believe that conventional warfare carried out in the Mus-

11. Michael Howard, *The Invention of Peace and the Reinvention of War* (London: Profile, 2001), p. 102.

12. Lind's Fourth Generation seminar, made up mostly of U.S. Marine Corps officers, recently published the first (unofficial) field manual on how to fight fourth-generation conflicts. Titled FMFM 1-A, *Fourth Generation War*, it is available on www.military.com and other Web sites.

lim world increases, rather than decreases, the threat to the American homeland by this new kind of warfare.[13]

America the Vulnerable

Major changes have already occurred within American society since 9/11. A year and a half after the U.S. Commission on National Security recommended to President Bush that he create a new homeland security agency and eight full months after 9/11, the president finally endorsed a Department of Homeland Security and it is in a continuing state of being organized. Billions of dollars, much of it unwisely spent, as demonstrated by the department's dilatory performance after Hurricane Katrina, are going into the effort to prevent attacks on America or respond to them when they occur.

The Patriot Act, containing controversial provisions for probably unconstitutional searches and seizures, was quickly passed. Internment camps at Guantanamo Bay, Cuba, and elsewhere have been established for prisoners captured in Afghanistan and Iraq, though how long they will be held, whether they are being held as prisoners of war, war criminals, or simply criminals, and to what degree of due process of law they are entitled have yet to be announced. Rumbles from the American judiciary, mindful of constitutional guarantees of due process, are finally being heard. "Detainees," an amorphous category without a context in the law, are treated neither as criminals, thus subject to the criminal justice system, nor as warriors, and thus subject to the Geneva Conventions and the international laws of war having to do with due process and prisoners' rights. And as I, among others, warned in 2002, the cost of this willful legal ambiguity was massive prisoner abuse, leading in many cases to death, at Abu Graib

13. Lind argues that in a fourth-generation world, America's grand strategy needs to be defensive, not offensive. See his cover story, "Strategic Defense Initiative," in the 22 November 2004 issue of the *American Conservative,* pp. 9–15.

and throughout the far-flung "detainee prison system." And though airport security has been intensified, borders and ports are still porous, and other means of transportation are virtually without security.

Curiously, though President Bush declared war on terrorism on September 20, 2001, the private sector of America, its critical infrastructure and means of production, has yet to be engaged in this war nationally. Special pleading and lobbying by the petrochemical and the railroad industries, among a number of others, have successfully prevented any legislation from passing that would require them to increase their security.

Though most of the valuable American targets and those most likely to damage our economy if attacked remain unsecured, corporate America has not been called upon to contribute to the war on terrorism nor to help provide increased security for its own vulnerable facilities, many of which are located in and around mass urban populations. Years after 9/11 and despite repeated warnings of future attacks, America lacks any sense of urgency regarding its own self-protective shield.[14]

Except in the rare case of the major false alarm in Iraq, few politicians, including presidents, are rewarded for alarming people, especially when time has passed, memories of riveting catastrophe have faded, routine life has continued, and citizens are led to believe or choose to believe that terrorists are being held at bay in Iraq. It is a comforting thought, indeed much more comforting than the awful contemplation of an imminent mass-casualty attack on other American cities.

But if William Lind and others are right that we now face a new kind of warfare, one carried out against civilian, not military, targets

14. See "America—Still Unprepared, Still in Danger," task force report of the Council on Foreign Relations, October 2002, available at www.cfr.org; Stephen Flynn, *America the Vulnerable: How Our Government Is Not Protecting Us from Terrorism* (New York: HarperCollins, 2004).

on the soil of the United States by nonstate actors (or stateless nations), actors who may already be inside the United States, then
whistling past the graveyard is a poor substitute for genuine security. The traditional military shield is increasingly ineffective against
fourth-generation warriors.

Occasionally, dramatic steps, usually on very special occasions
such as presidential inaugurations, are taken that acknowledge this
dangerous new reality. "Somewhere in the shadows of the White
House and the Capitol" during the January 20, 2005, inaugural, reported the *New York Times*, "a small group of super-secret commandos stood ready with state-of-the-art weaponry to swing into action
to protect the presidency."[15] Extraordinary activities such as this are
vivid and startling reminders of the age in which we live, the fragile
nature of security, not just for presidents, and the arrival of fourth-
generation warfare on American soil as a permanent reality of the
twenty-first century. The size of the commando operation was not
revealed, but it was part of an army of thirteen thousand federal
agents, Secret Service personnel, and law enforcement officers from
throughout the region committed to protect the inauguration of an
American president in the nation's capital on American soil.

Secretly deploying commandos at presidential inaugurals, however, is not without consequence. The news report cites a complica-
tion, one that penetrates to the core of the U.S. Constitution and
the founding framework of the republic. Following a national election in 1876 roughly as close as that of 2000, federal troops were called
out to put down any efforts to overturn that election. This action
frightened those familiar with the reasons for the Constitution's recognition of the militia (later, the states' National Guards) as the frontline of homeland defense and the founders' fear, based on their
understanding of the principles of the republican form of govern-

15. "Commandos Get Duty on U.S. Soil as Antiterrorism Efforts Expand," *New York Times*, January 23, 2005.

ment, of the use of regular military forces to enforce domestic laws. In response, in 1878, Congress passed the Posse Comitatus Act proscribing military forces from carrying out law enforcement duties.[16] Happily, the commandos were not called upon to act and their mobilization at the 2005 inaugural site was not disclosed until afterward, and, therefore, the issue of whether their use violated the Posse Comitatus Act did not arise, at least on that occasion.

But the incident does raise a question of considerable importance. Since the age of terrorism has no foreseeable ending, when there are further terrorist attacks on America, will our military forces be called upon to play an active, continuing, and visible role in the attempt to prevent those attacks and to respond to them? If so, and the answer is most likely "yes," will that not represent a major change in American society? The answer is also "yes." After 9/11, the sight of uniformed members of the National Guard, local citizen-soldiers, at airports caused many Americans to feel as uneasy as they were comforted. Instead of National Guardsmen and women, the sight of the Eighty-Second Airborne Division or the First Marine Division on the street corners of America would be even more disquieting, and rightly so.

This problem has been further exacerbated by the Bush administration's postmortem response to Hurricane Katrina. Instead of insisting that the Department of Homeland Security be better organized and managed, it has suggested that disaster response be turned over to the Pentagon—a serious challenge to the Constitution's prohibitions against the use of the standing army to enforce our domestic laws.

Fourth-generation warfare carried out over time on American soil represents a dramatic departure in the history of our national security. It is not simply a question of creating new kinds of military forces, equipping them differently, deploying them in new venues,

16. See Gary Hart, *The Minuteman: Restoring an Army of the People* (New York: Free Press, 1998), for a more detailed treatment.

and training them in counterinsurgency warfare, urban search-and-destroy missions, and even individual assassination assignments. It is a question of all this taking place on a continuing basis on the American homeland and within our society. The implications for the massive transformation of American society, almost entirely in an unpleasant even frightening way, are apparent. Since 1812, we have never had to erect our security shield on our own soil.

Mindful of the statutory restrictions on the deployment of regular military forces on American soil and the social transformation that would represent, another alternative, that of private security forces, has been quietly emerging. Well before 9/11, crime rates in major cities led to the expansion of the size, lethality, and authority of urban police forces.

Even so, with the capital city of Washington being one of the least secure cities in America, the privatization of security for business interests and individuals wealthy enough to afford it began to take place. In virtually every country, including the United States, one of the biggest growth industries is the private security business. Nation-states were formed in the seventeenth century around the bargain that nations (peoples) would grant the state (government) their loyalty in exchange for security. The privatization of security implies that the state is not keeping its side of the bargain either because it will not do so or, more likely, because it cannot do so.

At the very least, this opens up a massive social division between those who can provide for their own security and the vast majority who cannot. Even so, if fourth-generation warriors are clever enough to bring down the symbols of American capitalism, they will find a way to use biological or chemical agents to contaminate the food supplies of gated communities and wealthy suburban enclaves. That is, unless the private security forces also contract to do the shopping and taste the produce.

The contrast between the methods we are using, including pre-emptive warfare, larger armies with larger weapons, and freedom crusades, and the new realities of the world we live in, including nonstate actors, religious fundamentalism, and fourth-generation warfare on our homeland, could not be more stark. It is, in the memorable phrase of the historian Barbara Tuchman, "the march of folly."[17] In her account, folly is represented by a nation's pursuit of an inadequate or failed policy knowing that a better option is available. The enemies of progress, according to historian Arthur Schlesinger, Jr., have always been gravity (inertia), custom, and fear. Gravity and custom represent the traditional and known ways of doing things. Fear represents the resistance to that which is new or different.

We invaded Iraq under the pretext of a war on terrorism. In fact, we invaded Iraq to complete business left unfinished in Gulf War I, to create a political base in the greater Middle East, to help guarantee oil supplies, and simply because we believed that we would be uniformly welcomed by the Iraqi people. Conventional thinking prevented us from taking the necessary first step to achieving security in the twenty-first century—*thinking differently*. No one can seriously believe that terrorist cells already in the United States planning the next attacks are being deterred by our occupation of Iraq.

Like guerrilla warfare in the twentieth century, terrorism is a method used by those with a larger agenda. By and large, guerrilla warfare was fought on the native soil of the indigenous warriors to force colonial powers to leave, and it worked in virtually every case. Guerrilla warfare was waged to force colonial powers to question their values, to count the cost of their policies, and to think differently. It succeeded. Though U.S. interests, military and commercial, around the world are targets of value, the real war by terrorists against America is being, and will be, fought on American soil. Though the British and the Spanish have fought indigenous guer-

17. Barbara Tuchman, *The March of Folly: From Troy to Vietnam* (New York: Random House, 1984).

rilla organizations to a standstill on their homelands, no nation has as yet perfected the methods to defeat terrorism or to win a fourth-generation war. The first step in doing so is to think differently about security, to understand its new dimensions. It is not the same thing as it was during the recent Cold War.

Security's Many Layers

In January 2001, the U.S. Commission on National Security/21st Century, acknowledging that security in the new twenty-first century would be a much different undertaking than in the twentieth, laid out six objectives for U.S. national security. These objectives recognized, possibly for the first time officially, that security in the new century had to combine shield and cloak.

The first objective was to defend the United States and ensure that it is safe from the dangers of a new era. The commission recommended dramatic steps for prevention of, protection from, and response to looming terrorist attacks. New military, paramilitary, law enforcement, and intelligence capabilities were called for, and the reorganization and consolidation of disparate government agencies were strongly recommended.

But the commission also recognized a broader security reality. Increased investment was required in education, science, and technology to maintain America's social cohesion, economic competitiveness, and technological ingenuity, as well as its military strength. Further, U.S. security required the promotion of new regional centers of stability, particularly Russia, China, and India. Added to that was the expansion of global economic opportunity in the context of more effective international institutions and international law. Rather than pursue domination, the United States' urgent task is to strengthen international alliances so that America's partners assume greater autonomy and responsibility. And finally the United States is to help the international community resist the disintegrating changes brought on by globalization, state failure, mass migration, and proliferation of weapons of mass destruction. Behind our shield of military strength should be a cloak of common international security.

Central to this security strategy is a sense that we are not in this alone, that our security, in an age of global integration, is reliant on a global community—a commons—with increased opportunity and responsibility. This premise proved itself to be absolutely true when the dreaded warning of terrorist attacks and mass casualties on the American homeland proved accurate, and the world community supported our efforts to destroy its perpetrators in Afghanistan. Abandoning this common security agenda, as we did shortly thereafter, ignored the vital connection between American security and international cooperation in the twenty-first century.

Once we achieve the necessary stability in Afghanistan, and once we work our way out of the hornets' nest that is Iraq, we will then realize that revolutionary forces are transforming the character of war. This transformation therefore requires an equally revolutionary transformation in the nature of security. As threats are new, so new opportunities to counter those threats must be created. There are new ways to create a shield and new imperatives to create a cloak of security.

Three-Dimensional Threats and Opportunities

Opportunities Used to Reduce Threats

Despite the end of the Cold War, the world of the early twenty-first century may be even more dangerous and therefore more insecure than before. It is, of course, much too early to say. But this age is already characterized by a combination of epic changes that occurs rarely in human history. Laws, regulations, rules, governments, the very state itself were all devised to create predictability of human behavior and to control misbehavior. These are the walls that protect us from chaos and violence and thus represent our security. We feel secure when we walk out of doors in the morning and know what to expect. Insecurity is not knowing what to expect and therefore expecting the worst. At its core, insecurity is rooted in the loss of predictable safety.

New Causes of Insecurity

Let's consider the collection of new developments, almost all of them neutral on any security scale, which together create huge insecurities. Technology itself is at the top of the list. Technology as applied to destruction is producing increasing numbers of weapons capable of mass casualties and mass destruction of property. These are usually cataloged under one of three categories: nuclear, chemical, or biological. Nations have been using chemicals to poison each other's armies for at least a century. World War I enemies used mustard gas and similar munitions against each other wholesale. And the Nazis perfected, if that is the appropriate word, the use of chemicals for mass slaughter, at least of civilian noncombatants.

Nations have yet to use biology in the form of viral plagues or other maladies against each other, though testing and experimentation with such agents have been known to take place. In an age of suicidal terrorism, it is certainly quite easy to conceive of any number of attackers willingly infecting themselves with a highly toxic, highly contagious virus, say, smallpox, Ebola, Asian avian virus, or whatever, and fanning out through subway systems, sports events, and shopping malls in America to create epidemics. And Hiroshima and Nagasaki tell us all that we need to know about nuclear destruction in cities.

Technology is also miniaturizing and privatizing the manufacture of weapons of mass destruction. Until recently the province of nation-states, and those states by and large behaving responsibly, production of such weapons by nonstate actors in small laboratories, particularly in the case of biological weapons, is rapidly becoming more feasible.

In some ways, weapons of mass destruction represent dual threats: from their use and from the technology democratizing their production and ownership. This simply means that when the genie of mass destruction escapes the lamp, it cannot be put back in by nation-states negotiating treaties to do so. The political equation based on the post-Westphalian state monopoly on violence is being fundamentally and perhaps permanently altered by technology.

It is not accidental that this startling new reality coincides with the failure of states. When a state cannot guarantee the security of its citizens, the state's claim on the loyalty of its citizens is shattered. People then begin to look for their own means of security, usually through private armies, small associations, or private arms. Then reversion to feudalism accelerates. As previously noted, wealthy people can and are creating their own small armies in their suburban gated enclaves. Nonwealthy people must form their own security organizations, and they might well, for example, call them hunting clubs to be polite. Working-class people in urban centers will form similar organizations, perhaps in the form of neighborhood watch groups, but they will be only one step removed from the gangs which poor young people already have formed. Such scenarios could be easily dismissed as apocalyptic except for one fact: They are already happening.

It reflects an elemental fact of human nature. Human beings require some basic sense of security. Otherwise, life really is a jungle. And those who are able to do so, that is, everyone who is not too old, too young, too poor, or too isolated, will find some way to find security for themselves and their families, usually in small defined groups. The astronomical spiral of gun ownership in the United States, unmatched anywhere else in the world, is a tribute to this fact. It is also the most vivid testimony that a society can provide for its lack of confidence in its government and in that government's ability to protect its citizens. It will be a cause of wonder for future generations why the greatest power in the history of the world was, at the height of its powers, still populated by so many frightened people who found it necessary to arm themselves to the teeth. The most vociferous of the gun owners state the obvious conclusion bluntly: We do not trust our government. But that gun will not do much good against an insidious and calculating terrorist who slips anthrax into the local public school's cafeteria.

Together with technology making weapons of mass destruction available to all and states losing their monopoly on violence and their ability to provide security, other new realities are, or soon will be, threats to security. Mass migrations from Africa to Europe and from Latin America to the United States are fundamentally changing cultures and societies. Europe's Muslim population is exploding from such migrations and from its own huge birth rates. By 2020, one quarter of all American citizens will be Hispanic. Neither is, by itself, a bad thing. It is simply a different and very important thing. One kind of society swallows enough different people, and one day it becomes a different kind of society. It may or may not retain its historic values, beliefs, customs, and cultures. Probably not. But as this trend accelerates, the demographic, social, and political revolutions all around naturally create a sense of insecurity among those who find comfort in their traditional cultures.

Confronted with evidence of increasing numbers of private organizations producing weapons of mass destruction, the rise of private security forces, and visible, daily evidence of being enveloped by a demographic revolution, imagine a concerned working mother who sees a story headlined "Countdown to Global Catastrophe," which claims that a task force of senior politicians, business leaders, and scientists from around the world has just reported that "in as little as 10 years, or even less . . . the point of no return with global warming may have been reached leading to droughts, agricultural failure, water shortages, sea-level rise, and the death of forests."[1] Like most if not all of her fellow citizens, this woman's sense of insecurity is mounting.

Even though the threat of AIDS seemed to have been contained for the moment, albeit at a very high level, in the United States and most of Europe, it continues to decimate the populations of many Asian, African, and Latin countries. Almost as many people, particularly children, are dying of malaria in these same countries. Though these may seem distant threats to an uncontaminated American, they destabilize nations and whole economies and create almost unbear-

1. *Independent*, London, January 24, 2005.

able mountains of human misery. And they contribute to state failure. Into such voids flow religious fundamentalism, clans led by warlords, mafias seeking control of vital resources, and terrorist organizations offering identity and at least limited security to stateless, rootless, hopeless people.

Not all biological danger is man-made or man-spread. Virologists are concerned that highly contagious pathogens are capable of outrunning our efforts, even global efforts, to contain them. Almost a century ago, an influenza epidemic killed almost fifty million people worldwide before burning itself out. In the minds of some, the Asian bird flu, or avian virus, or any one of dozens of evolving versions of it represents at least the same potential. Commenting on the mounting threat from the bird flu virus, a World Health Organization official said, "We at WHO believe that the world is now in the gravest possible danger of a pandemic," a global pandemic that could kill millions.[2] Now, however, there are much more efficient delivery systems than a century ago. The human being remains the carrier.

Millions of human beings are circumnavigating the globe every day in thousands of aircraft. It would be ironic, to say the least, if the huge resources invested in the effort to prevent terrorist use of biological weapons were made redundant by Mother Nature. Even now, experts are complaining that the world community is totally lacking in a collective strategy to combat a viral pandemic. Perhaps the human mind, including the human political leader's mind, takes a Darwinian view of natural, as opposed to man-made, catastrophes and simply says that epidemics are as impossible to defend against as tsunamis, part of the human condition and not subject to serious human anticipation or response.

Any review of new risks and threats itself creates the danger of focusing too much on fear and danger and neglecting the good

2. "Official: Bird Flu Pandemic Is Imminent," Associated Press, *New York Times*, February 23, 2005.

things going on in the world. Balance requires the acknowledgment of marvelous breakthroughs in medicine, nations and regions with expanding economies and rising living standards, progress in democratic rights for women and for whole nations, and a wealth of similar evidence that the human race is not inevitably doomed. But any realistic effort to think about security in an age with new and different threats must focus analysis on those threats in order to be able to imagine ways of dealing with them. In an age of dramatic change, an ostrich with its head in the sand, though comforted for the moment, is probably going to be a dead ostrich.

New Opportunities

The proliferation of weapons of mass destruction by technology, the failure of states and the erosion of their traditional monopoly on violence, mass south-to-north migrations, global warming, and epidemics all represent the liability side of the early twenty-first-century ledger and the new causes and dimensions of insecurity. On the other side of the ledger, are there assets or opportunities that can be used to neutralize these threats and thereby increase security?

The answer is most certainly "yes," and some of these opportunities have been suggested already. The same technological genius that spreads the knowledge of how to make destructive weapons can devise ways of neutralizing them. During the Cold War, we learned that any defensive capability that was cheaper to produce than the offensive weapon it was designed to protect against would make that weapon obsolete. If you can deflect a ground-to-air missile or a heat-seeking torpedo with relatively inexpensive chaff, you have rendered those missiles or torpedoes useless. Your enemy will have little incentive to mass produce and deploy them knowing you've figured out an effective and inexpensive way to render them ineffective. This is, of course, the theory behind Star Wars and its renamed replacement, the national missile defense system. Except in this case, some cruel facts have murdered the beautiful theory. The defensive shield costs more than the missiles it is designed to defeat; the marginal costs far outweigh the marginal benefits; and it has failed to perform with sufficient reliability to make its immense costs worthwhile.

The same principle works the other way. During the 1970s, 1980s, and into the 1990s, the U.S. Navy built more than a dozen Nimitz-class aircraft carriers of more than ninety-five thousand tons each and carrying more than a hundred warplanes of various kinds. The total package cost for each carrier came to $10 billion or so, and that figure does not include the expensive escort ships in the armada, whose principal purpose is to protect the carrier. The difficulty is not that they can be sunk, which itself is more than theoretically possible, but rather that they can be disabled by a single torpedo costing perhaps $100,000. If a single such torpedo strikes the great ship's rudder and immobilizes it or if the ship can be caused to list only a few degrees and therefore be made incapable of launching and recovering its aircraft, the entire investment is rendered worthless. The investment-to-defeat ratio is way out of proportion.

This suggests that technology should now focus on how to make weapons of mass destruction less effective. For example, mass inoculations of vulnerable target populations against biological or chemical attack would help. The U.S. government proposed the inoculation of military troops and first responders against smallpox but then backed off because supplies were not readily available and a small percentage of people reacted negatively to the inoculation.

Widely dispersed early warning devices, so-called sniffers, can detect air- or water-borne chemical and nuclear agents and can be made to do so earlier and with more accuracy through further research and thus can save huge numbers of lives. Properly trained and equipped first responders, police, fire, and hazardous-material control teams, can evacuate and isolate areas contaminated by biological, chemical, or nuclear devices, thus substantially limiting the damage to people and property. This is particularly true for chemical agents, which are often difficult to disperse. This list of technological innovations is illustrative and should, of course, include many similar steps that reduce the effectiveness of weapons of mass destruction at least or make them worthless at best. The basic principle is always to look for ways to do so.

Technology does not offer a solution to the crisis of state legitimacy. But more effective law enforcement, more urgency in homeland security, more visible recognition of the new threats to security, and more creative and imaginative protective measures all could contribute to rebuilding citizen confidence in the state, to social cohesion, and to reducing the trend toward social atomization, private security forces, and the resort to vigilante self-protection. Resort to our constitutional heritage is also now required.

The U.S. Constitution's creation of two armies, the regular army and the citizen militia army, and the historical reason that the founders found this necessary is fascinating.[3] A hundred years ago, the constitutional militia became the National Guard, which is under the control of state governors until mobilized (or "federalized") into national service.

One reason has been mentioned: the fear of regular federal troops on the streets of America enforcing the laws, the first step, in the minds of the founders, toward dictatorship. But the second reason is the more interesting. The founders used the language of the republic, the theory of government devised by the Greeks in the fifth century B.C., and they purposely intended the new United States to be a republic. Even today, we pledge allegiance to the flag of the republic, though few Americans could say why. The founders' contribution to republican theory was to devise a federal republic composed of (eventually) fifty state republics.

3. See Gary Hart, *The Patriot: An Exhortation to Liberate America from the Barbarians* (New York: Free Press, 1996) and *The Minuteman: Restoring an Army of the People* (New York: Free Press, 1998).

With the possible exception of Switzerland, this had never been done in twenty-three hundred years. But one of the hallmarks of a republic is its reliance on citizen-soldiers: in the ancient Greek days, farmers who put down their plows and took up their spears and shields to protect the city-state republic. Not only was the citizen-soldier to be relied on to avoid a standing army becoming the instrument of a dictator, a "man on a white horse," but it also was the essence of civic virtue, the responsibility of the citizen to participate in the life of the republic, most vividly in its collective defense.

If security is now both a function and a definition of the commons, its first guarantors are its citizens.

Starting with my service on the Senate Armed Services Committee in the mid-1970s and for three decades since, I have championed the National Guard because of these historic and constitutional reasons. As a member of the U.S. Commission on National Security/21st Century in the 1990s, I strongly urged a policy of reliance on the National Guard as the centerpiece of homeland security. Now, as we contemplate terrorism and new threats to national security, the National Guard is a prime illustration of a policy that would strengthen the state and help to restore the legitimacy of the republic. People lose confidence in the state, or we would probably say the government, when they believe the government has lost confidence in them.

To be effective, however, the National Guard has to be available. Not only is the National Guard not available for prevention of terrorist attacks, it has also not been available for disaster response—as in the case of Hurricane Katrina—because it has been relocated to Iraq.

Government (not just national government but all government) has become increasingly professional and bureaucratic, with career politicians replacing citizen-politicians, and it believes that its role is to provide services from the top down rather than to engage citizens in self-government and their local communities. This is particularly true where public safety and security are concerned. As warfare became more professional, armies became more professional (and bureaucratic) and thus more remote from the people they protected. The end of conscription and the rise of the all-volunteer army in the mid-1970s signaled a historic shift in this regard. Further, technologically sophisticated weapons required highly trained operators. Emphasis was placed not only on the recruitment of volunteers but on the retention of those whose training was extremely expensive. Emphasis also shifted from citizen-soldiers defending their homeland to professional, technologically skilled warriors waging war in far-off places.

The gap that widened between the professional army and the citizens it protected also made it easier to commit the professional army to warfare with much less social and political cost than would have been the case with an army of conscripts and draftees. Whereas there were mass demonstrations during the draft-fed Vietnam War, there were many fewer demonstrations against Gulf War I or Gulf War II. War had become a distant thing carried out by professionals—that is, until war came to America's shores on 9/11.

The political gap between a professional army and ordinary citizens, the legal gap between regular forces and domestic law enforcement, and the constitutional gap between the regular army and the militia have all been placed under an intense spotlight by America's vulnerability to terrorism. That spotlight represents public insecurity and the erosion of citizen confidence in government's ability to provide security. Ironically, conservatives' lack of confidence in the government's ability to solve social inequities is now mirrored by the majority's lack of confidence in the government's ability to provide protection.

The age of terrorism offers new proof of the wisdom of the founders. If we do not want regular military forces on our streets, are there nevertheless those who can defend us? The answer is found in the constitutional provisions for a militia or National Guard. If we are waging war on terrorism, as President Bush has repeatedly proclaimed, why are the citizens of the American republic also not called upon to be soldiers in that war?

By enlisting America's citizens in this war, we would be empowered, we would have a role to play, and we might regain a measure of confidence in our government because we would be participants in its most important activity, providing security. Clearly, every able-bodied man and woman cannot join the National Guard. But the National Guard is now deployed in Iraq, far from our shores and far from being trained and equipped, as it should be, for homeland security. Because these citizen-soldiers are filling combat and combat support roles, and because their tours of duty are being repeatedly and involuntarily extended, the National Guard is hemorrhaging troops.

So, citizens concerned for their safety and willing and able to play a role in achieving security should be encouraged to join the National Guard. That has not happened. For tens of thousands of other Americans, auxiliary roles should be created. Ordinary citizens can be trained and equipped to become auxiliary first responders in case of catastrophe. They can help police forces and firefighters cordon off a disaster area and direct traffic. They can drive ambulances during mass-casualty attacks. They can play auxiliary medical roles in triage situations and perform elementary rescue and recovery roles. As citizen-soldiers, they form both shield and cloak.

Perhaps even more important, in an age when expeditionary war is increasingly being fought by highly trained professional specialists and conscription no longer demands service to the nation, the opportunity for citizen-soldiers to serve their country can be a much-needed force for social solidarity and unity. In the nineteenth and twentieth centuries, traditional national wars were a cohesive social force that brought our nation together. Now, new unconventional threats provide an opportunity for citizens to play an important role in the protection of our nation and in reconstituting the meaning of citizenship.

The Office of Citizen

Months before 9/11, the U.S. Commission on National Security/21st Century proposed "a national campaign to reinvigorate and enhance the prestige of service to the nation."[4] Several steps were proposed to implement this effort to draw the highest-quality citizens back into all avenues of national service. First, expanded educational assistance was proposed in exchange for military and civilian service. Second, self-defeating barriers to appointment to public office were proposed to be lowered and standards for qualification made more realistic. The president and Congress were to revise the appointment process "by reducing the impediments that have made high-level public service undesirable to many distinguished Americans." Third, the president was to overhaul the foreign service system to attract the best and brightest young people into diplomatic service. Fourth, the president was urged likewise to reform the civil service by strengthening its hiring process, professional education system, and programs for retention of career public servants. Fifth, the executive branch of government was urged to create a National Security Service Corps to ensure a corps of national security policy experts throughout the government. Sixth, Congress was urged to strengthen and expand the G.I. Bill and link service to educational opportunities for all of the services and to expand veterans' benefits to increase the recruitment and retention of the best military officers and troops. All of these recommendations had to do with the cloak of security.

4. *Road Map for National Security: Imperative for Change*, final report of the U.S. Commission on National Security/21st Century, Washington, D.C., January 31, 2001, p. 89.

The events of 9/11 require that threats be countered by exercising opportunities. Reasonable people might assume that this tragedy would have provided whatever additional impetus was required to cause the president and Congress to adopt these measures. In this case, reasonable people would be wrong. None of this, so important to better government and national security, has been done. Nor have extensive recommendations for improving national security by restructuring the executive branch, especially the Department of State, the Department of Defense, and the National Security Council, and Congress and its antediluvian committee structures even been discussed, let alone implemented. Though we have declared war on terrorism, we have only reluctantly created a Department of Homeland Security, and we have taken no steps whatsoever to empower regular citizens to help secure our country or to recruit the highest-caliber people in America to serve.

America's New Role in the World

If one believes, however, that security at home cannot be achieved without more creative thinking in the United States' dealings with the rest of the world—the crucial new dimensions on the global security chess board—then foreign policy initiatives also offer opportunities for increasing security. The number of failed and failing states must be confined. Fragile states must have help rebuilding themselves. Rogue states must be contained and isolated. Renegade nonstate actors must be denied roots in any country or support from any networks. Terrorists, drug cartels, mafias, and arms merchants must be isolated from each other and prevented from forming networks, subgovernments, and subcultures of their own. As powerful as it is, the United States cannot achieve any of these objectives, let alone all of them together, by itself. Some in power view U.S. "leadership" as dictatorial, dominating, and unilateral. Conceivably, these attitudes might work with the humblest of nations, some of which, for example, provided a diminished company of troops to the "coalition forces" invading Iraq, usually in exchange for a substantial increase in "foreign aid" (read: sophisticated bribery).

But that kind of leadership will not work with larger, more sophisticated, and more powerful nations, nor is it worthy of a truly great nation. Instead, leadership should mean the cooperative identification and achievement of mutual interests and common objectives. This often empowers the lesser nation and enables us to share the burden of addressing these new international sources of insecurity. The most visible and important potential countries for such an approach are Russia, China, and India, three key players on the security chess board of the twenty-first century. In varying degrees and in different circumstances, each represents an actual or potential regional power which, if properly encouraged by the United States, can play a role in shoring up and restructuring failing states, can contribute substantially to restricting the proliferation of weapons of mass destruction, can create productive regional trading blocs and stabilize economies, can reduce ethnic and religious tensions, can help to track down terrorists, and generally can play a greater political role than simply financing America's debt (China), providing a source of oil (Russia), or writing our software (India).

Barriers of prejudice in certain U.S. foreign policy circles must be overcome. Since the collapse of the Soviet Union and the end of the Cold War, some have sought to make China the successor enemy against which we can array our military and political power. This has proved difficult so far because China has yet to show any real animosity toward the United States or, save for Taiwan, any serious project to create hegemony (in the form of an Asian Warsaw Pact, for example) in its greater region. Indeed, it is hedged about by four powers, Russia, Japan, India, and to some degree Indonesia, which have shown little interest in falling under Chinese direction or control. Instead, China seems bent on creating the kind of capitalist market economy that many Americans claim to want for the world.

We are in fact encouraging China's move by buying many of its products and developing joint production ventures within China itself. In turn, China has become a major American creditor, buying our debt so that we can continue to consume Chinese products. We borrow money from them so we can buy what they produce. Whether this is as good a deal for us as it is for them depends on one's point of view. If one believes that debts have to be repaid sooner or later, then future generations of Americans may, like myself, not believe so.

In some part because of the lack of constructive U.S. policy since the end of the Cold War, Russia stagnates economically and slips backward politically. This did not have to happen. A Marshall Plan to reconstruct Russia in the 1990s, that included more serious efforts at political and economic institution building than were actually made, could have seen Russia in the twenty-first century in a much better position, one that could have put it strongly in the Western world and made it a more constructive power in its region. As with China, that is part of the problem with U.S. foreign policy. It turns out that a number of U.S. foreign policy shapers were not simply anticommunist; they were also anti-Russian. They did not want a successful, healthy Russia. They claimed to fear its quick restoration to power and eventual aggression. In fact, they were perpetuating ancient grievances brought over from nations bordering Russia. The major Western European powers have seemed only slightly more willing to welcome Russia into their midst.

Instead, U.S. policy seems to be to surround Russia with U.S. military bases and forces as close to its borders as possible. Even a passing knowledge of Russian history shows this to be counterproductive at best. Finger pointing serves no purpose at this point, except that history will view the post–Cold War period as a massive loss of opportunity by the United States to create a stable, progressive, democratic Russia, fully a Western partner and a helpful influence on its entire region, particularly the troubled Asian republics on its southern borders.

India, of course, represents a different and more hopeful opportunity. It is a mass democracy with an industrial and technological base that is, especially in the latter case, the envy of many. India has skillfully made itself into America's software writer and programmer and the out-source for much of the United States' data processing and storage. In many ways, this has proved to be a brilliant strategy and one that other nations might wish to emulate. India seems to be evolving a constructive relationship with China. Its greatest problem is Pakistan and the danger of the two nuclear powers losing control of their struggle over the contested regions of Kashmir and Jamu. Everyone views such an outcome as a catastrophe if not in the making then on the back burner. The United States should be encouraging India to play a wider and more constructive role in the region and should seek its help with the agenda of countering the proliferation of weapons of mass destruction, state building, regional trade development, population control, and terrorist hunting.

All of these suggestions apply as well to other nations in other regions, including Brazil, Mexico, Indonesia, Egypt, South Africa, South Korea, and a healthy number of others with evolving economies, at least some degree of democracy, regional influence, at least some resources, reasonably stable currencies, some educational structures, and varying degrees of political stability. As with Russia, China, and India, current U.S. policy toward most of these nations seems to be characterized by lassitude and an effort at best to maintain the status quo. There is little evidence that a foreign policy based on the exportation, or imposition, of freedom also includes a positive and constructive role for these and other nations in helping us to address the threats peculiar to the new century or to achieve the networks of international security required to make America secure.

The goal of expanding freedom leaves open the crucial question of *freedom to do what?* Is it freedom simply to vote, with the implication that this will lead to the possibility of at least a minimal livelihood? Is it freedom of the press, that is, for those who can buy one? Is it freedom to replace a repressive government, with no prospect that its successor will be any more capable of providing at least a little food and shelter? Is it, thus, freedom as an abstraction with no clear ties to prospects for a better life?

Are we preaching what Fareed Zakaria has insightfully called "illiberal democracy,"[5] the cover of respectability for authoritarian regimes bought by lopsided, virtually oppositionless elections, or is it true *liberal* democracy that includes the full range of constitutional rights and protections? The United States has to do better than preach abstractions about the kind of world in which we live if there is to be any hope of security for us and for other peoples. Great leaders, and great nations, rarely announce grand goals without some idea, some suggestion, some blueprint for how those goals are to be achieved. Otherwise, they are viewed by those in a world without hope as irrelevant or fraudulent.

Only some of the new sources of insecurity in the twenty-first-century world have been suggested here. Technology as applied to the ease of mass destruction, failing states and nations, the privatization of security, mass migration, global warming and climate change, pandemics—all are but illustrations of the barriers that any new security effort faces. They also all have one thing in common: None can be successfully addressed by a single nation, including the most powerful nation, alone.

Security of the Commons

The opposite approach is to *identify the elements of a common security cloak, to identify security as a collective objective, to empower other nations* and encourage them to assume portions of the burden either

5. Fareed Zakaria, *The Future of Freedom: Illiberal Democracy at Home and Abroad* (New York: Norton, 2003).

in their regions or according to their special capabilities; *to reduce the causes of violence* and isolate its agents; *to link ideals such as freedom and liberal democracy to real progress in the human condition* and thus make them worthwhile objectives not abstractions; *to use military power as a last not a first resort*; and perhaps most of all *to apply consistent standards to U.S. policy* so that our own interests, in oil, in borrowing, and in the use of other nation's military forces, do not require us to compromise our principles and make us hypocrites in the eyes of the world.

Following the end of the Cold War in 1991, and particularly since September 11, 2001, the United States has more often than not taken its unipolar, single superpower status to mean that the world has no choice but to follow us, that it is our way or the highway. The facts suggest that this attitude is swiftly becoming illusory. The European Union is consolidating its political and economic power and is beginning to discuss a collective defense strategy, with its own rapid deployment capability, separate and apart from that of the U.S.-led NATO. Led by China, Japan, and South Korea, East Asia is forming the largest trading bloc in the world, without U.S. participation or even U.S. consultation. And U.S. domination of the next frontier of space, for military and communications purposes, is being challenged by Europe in cooperation with China.

The more the United States goes it alone, with the expectation that the rest of the world has no choice but to follow, the more the rest of the world is beginning to prove otherwise. Instead of ignoring the aspirations of other nations and collections of nations, we should encourage them. Otherwise, we will soon find ourselves in the unenviable position of being the world's cop, troubleshooter, shield, and target, while other nations collectively pursue the cloak of better and more-productive lives.[6]

6. For an excellent exposition of this thesis, see Michael Lind, "How the U.S. Became the World's Dispensable Nation," *Financial Times*, January 25, 2005.

Leadership is by example, not dictation, and the examples we give the world are produced at home. The United States is the last Western democratic country to maintain and expand the death penalty, even as we preach human rights abroad. We preach laissez-faire (what Europeans call liberal) economic policies to developing nations, even as one in five American children lives in poverty. We advocate freedom and democracy throughout the world, even as half of eligible Americans choose not to vote. We purport to stand for transparency in politics, even as money delivered by special interest lobbyists dominates our election process. We proclaim transparency and the accountability of elected officials, even as our administration refuses to reveal to the public the names of those private interests that make our energy policy. We stand for the rule of law and an independent judiciary, even as systematic efforts are under way to stack the American courts with doctrinaire judges who are preapproved by conservative religious organizations. All this and more transpires as if hidden from the world, yet it all occurs in an age of instant and widespread information, including information about the conduct of the superpower. A message to Americans: People watch what we do much more than they listen to what we say.

To explore new methods of threat reduction—"drying up the terrorist swamp" is one colorful metaphor—requires international alliances and an American example. The first has a better chance of achievement if accompanied by the second. If globalization is made inclusive and expanded to developing and undeveloped nations, it can be a great opportunity to replace hopelessness with hope. Likewise, if access to information technologies held by advanced societies is shared, it will narrow the gap between advancing nations and the rest of the world and can revolutionize lagging national economies.

In many ways, success in achieving security in the early twenty-first century will be measured by the imagination shown by the United States and nations of good will in inventing opportunities to convert global revolutions into threat-reduction policies for the

THE SHIELD AND THE CLOAK

commons. Information technologies, such as low-cost wireless communications, can transform even the most rural economies and help markets to develop. In the 1990s, I helped a major U.S. telecommunications company to develop telecommunications projects in Eastern European and post-Soviet markets and helped to overcome political hurdles in order to pioneer in these regions. The transformative impact of modern, especially wireless, communications was demonstrated in Hungary, Czechoslovakia, Poland, and other Eastern European Soviet satellites in the late 1980s and early 1990s, when advanced Western communications systems, quickly installed, revolutionized stagnant economies and created vital urban and rural markets.

Likewise, energy devices based on solar, thermal steam, wind, and other renewable resources can provide immediate energy supplies even to remote areas of Asia, Africa, and Latin America and provide modest electrical systems to power small-scale industries and even reduce reliance on unstable supplies of oil in more advanced economies. Medical and biological breakthroughs much more widely disseminated to undeveloped areas can reduce infant mortality, thus leading to lower birth rates, prevent or control epidemics, and provide hope. Inexpensive water purification devices can revolutionize life in thousands of villages worldwide and slow mass migrations to urban slums. All these, and many more ideas, are but illustrations of what modern technology can do to create opportunities and to reduce risks of instability.

Life and Risk

As twenty-first-century insecurity cannot be defined simply by life-threatening dangers, it can also not be defined so broadly as to encompass every source of unease or discomfort. *Security is not perfect contentment, nor is insecurity caused only by the threat of terrorist attack*, as Hurricane Katrina painfully taught us. Having eliminated, at least for the foreseeable future, the likelihood of a nuclear exchange with Russia, we have found the world full of new and different challenges to our security. The search for security in this environment cannot become a paranoid enterprise that sees dangers everywhere. On the other hand, we do have to get beyond the notion that the capture of Osama bin Laden will produce a new nirvana. A certain amount of risk is inherent in the human condition. Security is, at least in part, the reduction of risk where it can be reduced and the elimination of the causes of risk where it is practicable to do so.

It is this effort that requires maximum imagination and collaboration among nations. During the Cold War years, attention was given to what were called "confidence-building measures" and "threat-reduction" steps. These varied from the periodic opening of the covers of missile silos to satellite inspection by the opponent so that numbers of missiles could be counted to eventual on-site inspection trips between the United States and the Soviet Union. To the degree that an autocratic or rogue state is believed to be developing a nuclear weapons capability or even a nuclear capability that could be converted to weapons production, international inspection is crucial. This is the current sticking point with both Iran and North Korea. Whereas critics argued that U.N. inspections in Iraq were inadequate and unreliable and, therefore, that hidden caches of weapons of mass destruction required invasion, it later turned out that the inspections were valid and accurate, and no such caches existed. Saddam Hussein found it impossible to prove that he did not have something he did not have, though he certainly could have been a lot more cooperative with U.N. resolutions requiring continued inspections.

To the degree that international institutions such as the United Nations can convince reclusive regimes to accept twenty-first-century confidence-building measures, including particularly comprehensive and unconfined inspections, to the same degree will the doctrine of preemption be less relevant. This still leaves the problem of regimes harboring evil-doers. The right of preemption can be declared where nations protect terrorist groups with the established intent to launch attacks on the United States or its allies whether or not it can be established that those groups have the means, in the form of weapons of mass destruction, to do so. Even so, the newly elected government of Afghanistan does not choose to harbor bin Laden, yet he is believed to be there still. There is a great difference between countries that provide haven to terrorists wittingly and those who do so either against their wishes or unwittingly.

There is a direct correlation between a nation's willingness to open its doors to other nations and the degree to which it is seen as a threat to others. Every nation has secrets even from its closest allies and friends. There are very large parts of the United States that are not only inaccessible to friendly foreigners but also to our own people. These include the most highly secret weapons-testing and -production facilities in the world. Suppose Iran or any other nation became paranoid about U.S. intentions. Is there any prospect that those facilities would be opened to U.N. inspectors? Not likely. Iran can claim, with at least a degree of plausibility, given statements by senior U.S. officials, that the United States is preparing to attack it. Throughout the Cold War, the United States took elaborate steps to conceal from the Soviet Union and others the size of its arsenal, the places where it was deployed, the capability of its weapons, and even its intention concerning their possible use.

Remember Richard Nixon's famous statement that he hoped the North Vietnamese would think that he was at least partially crazy and therefore, presumably, capable of anything? This is an extreme example of a traditional principle: The United States and other nations throughout history have understood the contribution to deterrence made by the lack of certainty on the part of its foes regarding its capabilities and its intentions. Yet, there is a limit to our ability to say, simply because we are a nation of self-professed good will, that we choose to act in concealment but that others about whom we have concerns cannot. It would certainly be interesting if we were to say to the Iranians, "You let us visit your nuclear facilities, and we will let you visit ours." This will not happen. But the price of uncertainty is further insecurity.

The security of the commons in the future will be achieved in direct proportion to our ingenuity in reducing the causes of insecurity. It is possible to use technology, globalization and trade, the communications revolution, and modern science to improve the lives of billions. It is possible to stabilize fragile states and improve economies, thus reducing the causes of mass migration. It is possible, at least for a few years to come, to reverse dangerous climate change. It is possible to control epidemics and attack new and old diseases. It is possible to bring the vast majority of the global population committed to good will closer together and further isolate and suppress radical fundamentalists, suicidal zealots, and forces of destruction and death. It is possible dramatically to reduce the proliferation of destructive technologies. These and many other historic achievements, some not conceivable before, are all now possible.

Clearly, rooting out terrorist cells and networks is a challenge for security forces, but even these are most often special branches of police forces and intelligence services rather than large-scale military combat forces. This, the most clear and present danger to U.S. national security, requires intense information sharing, international collaboration of a high order, and collective political will.

The hard part is not in knowing what must be done and how to do it; the hard part is generating the political will to do what must be done.

Applying Our Powers to the Purpose of Security

IV

S trategy is the application of our nation's powers to our large purposes. Achieving the shield and cloak of security is our first and
foremost purpose. What are the powers available to us and how do
we apply them to achieve the purpose of security?

In a previous book, *The Fourth Power: A Grand Strategy for the
United States in the 21st Century*,[1] I argued that America has three
traditional powers, economic, political, and military, each far superior to any other rival or nation, and that our large purposes should
be to achieve security for ourselves and friendly nations, to expand
opportunity for ourselves and others, and to promote liberal democracy where it does not now exist. I argued further that the United
States, given its unique constitutional history, possesses an unusual
fourth power, the power of the principles upon which our Constitution and system of government are based, which attracts the peoples
of the world. When we pursue policies based on these principles, we

---

1. New York: Oxford University Press (2004).

are most successful, and when we neglect or violate these principles out of short-term expediency, we weaken ourselves.

Our Principles and Security

During the Cold War, expediency too often led us to put our principles aside in the interest of thwarting the Soviet Union, overthrowing uncooperative governments, undermining democratic opposition to dictators who happened to be friendly to us, and even attempting to assassinate foreign leaders who would not cooperate. In virtually every case, our unprincipled actions failed and usually backfired, causing us to hurt the democratic cause we claimed to be pursuing.

Having served on the Senate Select Committee to Investigate the Intelligence Agencies of the United States (the so-called Church committee) in 1975 and 1976, I participated in the exposure of many of these excesses—including assassination plots against Fidel Castro, Patrice Lumumba, Ngo Dinh Diem, and several others, and the overthrow of democratically elected governments in Latin America and elsewhere—and had to face the dismay of my Colorado constituents, many of them idealistic students, and many others around the country who suddenly were confronted with the fact that the government whose flag they saluted had behaved a good deal nastier than they had been taught it was supposed to. In every case of abuse of the Constitution and violation of America's principles, the excuse given was that we were fighting a nasty opponent, the Soviet communists, and sometimes that required us to be just as nasty.

I was naïve enough then and am still idealistic enough today to believe this argument to be fundamentally wrong. It is one thing to listen to communications among Soviet leaders; it is quite another to hire Mafia assassins to rid us of troublesome, but otherwise powerless, political leaders. The issue is not simply occasional bad behavior, like some national Huck Finn running away from strict Aunt Polly. It is the willingness of our government, at least under some presidents, to violate our core national character, who we are and who we claim to be. This was shocking to a young senator, and it is disturbing still. Nor, sadly, was this kind of behavior exposed and then eliminated, never to return. Within ten short years after the Church committee exposed these un-American activities and sought to make future presidents accountable if they ever tried them again, the Reagan administration undertook the illegal and unconstitutional Iran-Contra program and then compounded this abuse of power by lying about it to Congress and the American people. Though "national security" was the predictable excuse given for this bizarre project, and the lies about it justified on the same grounds, like the secret (and illegal) bombing of Cambodia during the Nixon years, the purpose was not to keep the activity secret from those being attacked (the helpless Cambodians certainly knew they were being bombed, and the Central Americans knew our government was up to its eyeballs in their local conflicts), it was to keep these activities secret *from the American people.*

Democracy breaks down when government loses confidence in the people, or seeks to muster public support for devious and usually illegal activity, and the people then lose confidence in their government. That is the cost of unprincipled behavior that must be kept secret: the loss of public confidence in government. Expediency is the enemy of principle. To be a nation of laws not of men is to be committed to open and honest government, accountability of leadership, and the ability of the people to know what is right and what is wrong. There was a time when I heard chanted like a mantra, "Unless you want it on the front page of the *Washington Post*, don't do it," regarding one's personal life. Curiously, many of those doing the chanting were up to conduct regarding the public's business that they most certainly did not want on the front page of the *Washington Post*.

The first principle underlying a national security strategy, then, should be *the willingness and ability of government to justify its activities and conduct in pursuit of security before the American people in the court of public opinion.* Hard-liners and pragmatists will find this notion amusing and possibly even quaint. It's a dirty world out there, is their premise, and sometimes we have to do dirty things to protect ourselves. This idea may or may not be true, but it is certainly appealing to those who view the world in Hobbesian terms—that life is "nasty, brutish, and short." They take comfort in tough behavior even when it isn't called for, because, apparently the theory goes, if you are willing to be tough when you don't need to be—let's say by gratuitously torturing shackled prisoners—you'll really be tough when you have to be. There is more than a little of the maniacal missionary approach to the notion that we may have to torture you just a bit in order for you to see things our way and accept our faith which is, by all means, meant to save your soul.

The Inquisition was up to something along these lines.

Thinking Differently: Military Reform

Frustrated with a stale "spend more versus spend less" debate in the Senate on defense issues and the arms bazaar approach to weapons procurement ("five hundred of those and a thousand of these"), I pursued a movement called military reform being organized around the ideas of John Boyd, a retired air force pilot who applied a way of thinking about air-to-air combat to the notion of security and defense writ large. Grossly oversimplified, Colonel Boyd's theory applied what he called the "OODA loop" to military combat. OODA stands for observation, orientation, decision, and action. First, the opponent is observed: Where is he, where is he going, how is he going about getting there, and how fast? Once observation is completed, you must orient yourself to be in a favorable and commanding position over your opponent. Once you have successfully oriented yourself, you then decide what action to take: Lock on radar and fire air-to-air missiles, fire guns, stay in position and preserve options, or break off? Once the decision is made and action is taken, you assess the effects of your decision and prepare to repeat the loop by observing your circumstances.

The military reform approach to defense essentially stood the stale debate focused on weapons on its head. Instead of spending 95 percent of Congress's time analyzing, being lobbied about, and choosing weapons, those of us who founded the military reform caucus in Congress in 1980 took a different approach. People, not weapons, win wars. Unless the forces are properly trained and organized, even the most superior weapons will not guarantee victory in battle. Troops who know each other fight best. In the heat of battle, soldiers fight for their buddies more than their country. Yet, the United States was rotating troops in and out of units faster than any other military in the world. The British regimental system was the better model. Put people together and keep them together so they get to know and depend on each other. Officers were being promoted for having checked off certain career boxes on their résumés and having passed through expected bureaucratic hoops. Instead, military reformers said, officers who have demonstrated imagination and initiative in battlefield commands should be promoted fastest because they will be the strongest and most successful leaders during conflict.

After these kinds of personnel policies are adopted, then strategies, tactics, and doctrine are most important. A strategy based on attrition will fail, but a strategy based on maneuver warfare, outflanking and cutting off your enemy, will succeed much better. Only after getting the proper strategies, and the tactics and doctrines that follow, is it possible to determine what weapons to buy to fulfill those strategies and conduct proper operational doctrine. This represented a totally new way for members of Congress to think about the job of defense and to approach national security, and it had considerable impact particularly among newer members of the House and Senate on how they went about their jobs of authorizing and appropriating money for the military. All of this is to suggest another axiom upon which to build a new national security strategy: *You must properly understand what security is and how it is to be achieved, or all the military spending in the world will not make you more secure.*

Civic Membership

Creating a military along these reform lines, one that is shaped, focused, and trained for the conflicts of the future, is crucial to the security shield. Behind that shield, however, must be citizens who see themselves as part of a nation, who share the cloak of civic responsibility and civic membership.

A great debate opened in early 2005, but soon began to disintegrate, regarding America's core retirement plan, the Social Security system. Adopted during the precarious Depression era to provide at least a minimal financial safety net for all older Americans, its title was not chosen by accident. Franklin Roosevelt and those who voted with him were precise in their belief that genuine security required at least a small cushion of predictable and dependable financial support in retirement years. It was also called "social," which is partly the cause for the obsessive desire on the part of conservative forces for more than six decades to demolish it. Add "ism" to it and you get the point. Despite the fact that all working people, rich and poor, contribute to the system and that it is therefore not a handout, and despite the minimal but important help it has provided for hundreds of millions of Americans over those more than six decades, and despite the liberty it has provided for those millions to live independently of children and relatives, to the doctrinaire conservatives Social Security has always been the symbolic representation of big government and therefore a program to be despised.

Given its popularity, however, it could not simply be stamped out. A crisis had to be devised and the promise of greater wealth substituted to justify a camel's-nose-in-the-tent approach to its privatization and eventual destruction. Those ostensibly dedicated to "fiscal responsibility" used massive tax cuts in the 1980s and in the early twenty-first century in order to justify large-scale reductions in virtually all social programs. The Cold War secret policy world soon had its counterpart in domestic affairs where the true reasons for major shifts in values were not candidly given to the public. Most experts believe there is no crisis in Social Security financing or that if one might arise, it is several decades away. And behind the rhetorical shield of "ownership societies" and "financial empowerment" lurks the nasty little truth that equities markets can and do go down as well as up.

Pursued to its logical, and secret, extreme, this policy will lead to the Social Security system meeting its demise at the hands of the ever-patient conservatives. Very soon thereafter, hard-pressed working people will find it impossible to save, fortune will be unkind to the investments of many people, more and more elderly people will crowd themselves into the homes of their children and grandchildren, and another depression or serious recession will find many others destitute. Hopefully, another Franklin Roosevelt can once again be found to convince the American people that we really are all in this together, that we are a society with some attributes of family, that pulling together is more effective than pulling apart, that the gilded hope of every-man-a-millionaire is some ways off, and a new Social Security system will be reborn. And, like its predecessor, it will be, as Benjamin Barber has written, "an emblem of civic membership and a reflection of the benefits that come with the responsibilities of citizenship."[2] Instead of destroying the few remaining emblems of civic membership in an age of new insecurities, we should be looking for more of them. Civic membership forms the woven pattern in the cloak of security.

In the meantime, there is a principle of national security to be drawn from this epic ideological struggle: *Security means more than*

2. Benjamin Barber, "Privatizing Social Security: 'Me' over 'We,'" *Los Angeles Times*, January 27, 2005.

safety from attack, and each of us is more secure when all of us are more secure. The bonds of civic membership are crucial to a secure society and should be strengthened rather than weakened. The more you and I see ourselves as part of a greater American society with a sense of the commonwealth and the common good rather than each of us fighting an insecure world on our own, the more we will look for ways to incorporate security into that sense of commonwealth and seek ways to help each other achieve it. Systems like Social Security not only fulfill the purpose for which they were created, security in retirement, they also remind us that we are a republic based on popular sovereignty and on a sense of civic duty that requires us to look out for each other.

A nation of people who see themselves without common concerns and common solutions for those concerns, whose sense of community is blunted by privatization and atomization, is a nation that will find it difficult to fashion a sense of common security.

Extending Security's Reach

Using principles such as civic membership as a foundation, the pieces of a new security structure begin to appear. The U.S. Commission on National Security chose early in its deliberations to define security more broadly—to include cloak with shield—than in the narrow military sense inherited from the Cold War. Our equal numbers of progressive and conservative members understood that a mighty army and a weak government, or better weapons and worse schools, or greater firepower and a rejection of public service made no sense. So our reports urged a major increase in education investment, particularly in the sciences and mathematics, as necessary to a prosperous information-age economy and as the basis for a strong and secure nation. After creation of a new national homeland security agency, recapitalizing America's strengths in science and education was the next highest priority. "The scale and nature of the ongoing revolution in science and technology, and what this implies for the quality of human capital in the 21st century, pose critical national security challenges for the United States," we advised the new Bush administration. "Second only to a weapon of mass destruction detonating in an American city, we can think of nothing more dangerous than a failure to manage properly science, technology, and education for the common good over the next quarter century."[3]

Strong words, but carefully chosen. We found that the United States' need for the highest quality human capital in science, mathematics, and engineering is not being met. And we argued that this is not merely an issue of national pride or international image; it is an issue of fundamental importance to national security. Despite our calls on the president and Congress to double the U.S. government's investment in science and technology by 2010, five years later we have not even begun. We found that 34 percent of public school math teachers and almost 40 percent of science teachers lack even an academic minor in their primary teaching fields. We proposed an additional 240,000 teachers of science and math in elementary and high schools. It has not been done.

In 1997, Asia accounted for more than 43 percent of all science and engineering degrees granted worldwide, Europe 34 percent, and North America only 23 percent. During that same year, China produced 148,000 engineers to the United States' 63,000. We urged more scholarships for science and engineering students. Five years later, we have yet to make a start. We proposed detailed plans for scholarships and low-interest education loans, forgiveness of student debts for those entering military or government service, a national security teaching program to train very large numbers of new teachers, and the financing of professional development and lifelong learning—all in the national security interest. None of this has been done.

3. U.S. Commission on National Security/21st Century, *Road Map for National Security: Imperative for Change*, Washington, D.C., January 31, 2001.

We linked education to economic prosperity, economic prosperity to national security, and national security strength to world leadership. This divergence between stark new realities and our lack of response to them illustrates the central point of this argument: *Either we understand the new dimensions of security or we are doomed to insecurity and eventual decline.*

Beyond doubt, China's inevitable challenge to U.S. economic and therefore political leadership will be seen by those today who refuse to take the steps necessary to guarantee our vitality as Chinese aggression rather than American lassitude.

Where does the money come from for ambitious national investment in human capital, it will be asked, especially in a period of huge public deficits? The most direct answer is through changing our financial priorities. We are a debtor nation on a massive scale. Not only does our government run gigantic deficits almost like a profligate drunk, but individual and household debt is at historic highs, and corporations go through repeated cycles of borrowing for mergers, acquisitions, and consolidations that are more about the size of corporate egos than corporate efficiency. All of us borrow a lot of money. It is one thing to borrow money for investment, though there are strict limits on this practice to prevent speculation and bankruptcy, or to borrow for education or to finance a house. It is an entirely different thing to borrow money for consumption, especially for unnecessary consumption. In an age of cheap money, easy credit, and tantalizing advertising, deferred gratification is an antique and whimsical notion.

Were America to undertake to transform itself from a debtor to a creditor nation and from a consumption-based economy to a production-based economy through political leadership and major changes in tax incentives for savings and investment rather than for second homes and Humvees, there would be capital aplenty for rebuilding our education base in the national security interest. A consumption-based economy is insidious. In living memory, there was a time when households were divided between those that had a refrigerator and those that did not. Then, when all had a refrigerator, the division was between those that did and those that did not have television sets. Today, many households have multiple refrigerators and television sets in every room. And great advertising campaigns are launched to have them all replaced by this year's newest model, which has more technical gadgets. High school parking lots are full of cars, student cars, where in former years, the schools' small parking lots were for teachers and there were bicycle racks for students.

The response to the question "why not?" is pretty direct. Money spent is money not saved. Personal savings rates in the United States are abysmal. Because we don't save and because, even worse, we borrow to afford all those refrigerators, televisions, and cars, someone has to loan us the money. The problem is compounded by the public sector, the government, running monster deficits and also financing them with borrowed money. The two primary lender groups for private and public debt are foreigners and our children. In both cases, borrowed money is not free. It must be repaid and interest payments made in the meantime. Credit card interest payments for individuals and interest payments on government debt are both astronomical.

What does all this have to do with security? A debtor is rarely secure. In olden times, when debt was taken seriously, debtors unable to make repayment certainly could borrow no more money and usually went to prison. Today, they simply declare bankruptcy, and shortly several new unsolicited credit cards arrive in the mail. As to the U.S. government, "Central banks are shifting reserves away from the U.S. and towards the eurozone in a move that looks set to deepen the Bush administration's difficulties in financing its ballooning current accounts deficit," a deficit projected to reach $694 billion in 2005.[4] Even if one

4. Chris Giles, "Central Banks Shift Reserves Away from US," *Financial Times*, January 24, 2005.

believes, as the current administration's vice president seems to, that "deficits don't matter," that we can borrow endlessly from our children and future generations, there is still the problem of foreign lenders who see the value of debt-ridden dollars falling and choose not to lend the United States money by buying them.

Even if you insist on the old definition of security as exclusively a military concern, there are serious problems. Almost $500 billion of America's borrowing goes to its military forces and, if the costs of Iraq reconstruction as part of the war on terrorism are added in, it is well over $600 billion. If the central banks of the world think our currency is not worth holding, where do we get the money for ships, planes, tanks, soldiers' salaries, ammunition, and fuel and the costs of the occupation and rebuilding of Iraq? Where indeed do we get the money for homeland security? If we were to adopt a broader definition of security as threat reduction through creative internationalism, the problem becomes even larger. Where will the money come from for the U.S. share of international projects, such as childhood inoculations, local water and energy development, new communications systems, and hundreds of other projects to reduce the hopelessness that encourages violence?

By becoming a saving, investing, and producing nation, rather than a borrowing and consuming nation, we would sell more than we buy, we would reduce our dependence on others, the dollar would become sound, and we could afford to invest in future security. Much political rhetoric has been directed at "family values," "core values," and "society's values" in recent times. None of it has included the moral value of living within your means and not stealing from your children. The chickens coming home to roost at the height of America's drunken debt binge suggest a guiding principle for future security: *To be able to finance our future security, we must fundamentally change our national values and life styles, replacing consumption with production.*

So far, then, the principles upon which a new strategy for the security of the commons should be based include: confidence in govcrnment based upon the government trusting the people; the use of military reform principles to redefine what military security really is and how to achieve it; the notion of civic membership as the instrument of social cohesion; investment in our knowledge base to ensure American leadership; and replacing consumption with production as the basis of a sound economy.

The Changing Role of Military Power

All of this, of course, assumes that we have the military power and superior intelligence required to know how, when, and where to use it when our nation is threatened by those who wish to harm us. These capabilities will remain at the core of our security shield. The U.S. Commission on National Security concluded in its first report on September 15, 1999, that "the essence of war will not change,"[5] and that was true so far as it went, particularly if by "essence" we understand bloody and violent. The potential for conflict between nation-states, though declining, will be there as far into the future as we can see. And when it occurs, as in Iraq in 2003, superior force and maneuver will prevail. But wars of occupation, such as in Afghanistan and Iraq after the conventional "victories," offer a different challenge. These are low- or medium-intensity conflicts against insurgencies resembling cancerous cells using low-tech weapons, sometimes in suicidal fashion.

Belatedly, the Pentagon announced that it was outlining plans "for an ambitious reshaping of U.S. forces that would put less emphasis on waging conventional warfare and more on dealing with insurgencies, terrorist networks, failed states and other non-traditional threats."[6]

5. "New World Coming," U.S. Commission on National Security/21st Century, September 15, 1999.

6. Bradley Graham, "Pentagon Prepares to Rethink Focus on Conventional Warfare: New Emphasis on Insurgencies and Terrorism Is Planned," *Washington Post*, January 26, 2005.

It is important to note that this is not a massive program currently under way but is instead merely a sketch of a proposal to create a plan to undertake a change in direction that will takes years if not decades to achieve. This, four years after 9/11 and almost two years after the occupation of Iraq turned into a nightmare due to the lack of preparation for an insurgency war. The underlying principle seems to be not to adopt major military reforms until circumstances, such as bloody occupations, force you to question your thinking about the world in which you live and in which you fight. In any case, better late than never. During the Cold War, our strategy was the containment of Soviet communism. In the 1990s, it centered on fighting two regional wars simultaneously: in the Persian Gulf and on the Korean peninsula. After 9/11, our strategy, limited in imagination, became a war on terrorism carried out by preemptive and preventive wars of invasion.

The ambitious "reshaping" of America's strategy and its military forces required to carry it out will not be easy. This is true because of military service "unions," the political power of defense contractors, the gravity of traditional weapons planned or already in the procurement pipeline, and the stranglehold of memory. The big army is composed of officers who want ten or more combat divisions with heavy armor trained and equipped to fight and win a big conventional war and who resist, even in their own ranks, those who favor smaller brigades and faster, lighter units, such as the Rangers, as the forces of the future. Likewise, the surface navy organized around the big carriers and therefore stuck with at least some of them for another four decades or more will not be interested in rapid insertion and interdiction missions requiring smaller, faster, lighter, and lower-tech craft. The air force wants another (and presumably beyond that another) generation of high-performance combat aircraft loaded with the latest supertechnology even though the combat zones of the future will harbor nonstate actors whose airpower will consist only of those civilian airliners they can hijack and fly into tall buildings and high-value targets.

Military contractors make more money on heavy-duty, high-tech, supercapable weapons systems and will part with them reluctantly to say the least. Parts of each of these systems, as is now well understood, are produced in states and congressional districts all over the country to create jobs and therefore create constituency and congressional support, regardless of the true military value of the expensive weapons. Many of these weapons made redundant by insurgency warfare are already in production and therefore almost as costly to the taxpayers to shut down as to produce.

For these reasons, the belated shift in strategy and military structures will not be easy even for a president and Congress of the same party. Fast fighters, giant carriers, monster tanks, big missiles are all easier symbols of security than the new and much less dramatic needs that the Pentagon has recently discovered, including human intelligence gathering, foreign-language translators, constabulary (military police and peace keeper) forces, civil affairs experts to build communities, computer-network defenses, small pilotless aircraft drones, biological and chemical protection gear, and most of all a dramatic increase in special operations forces equipped and trained to fight the battles of the twenty-first, rather than of the twentieth, century.

The symbol of such forces is Delta Force and CIA personnel dressed in native garb riding donkeys in Afghanistan. When the cities of Iraq erupted in resistance following the announcement of "mission accomplished," it suddenly became obvious that we needed all of these things, and more, and we had virtually none of them. Our belated efforts to produce desperately needed body armor and vehicle armor for occupation forces in Iraq have been pathetic, even disastrous.

Necessity may prove to be the great reform motivator. Two years after what was proclaimed as a military "victory" in Iraq:

Unexpectedly heavy demands of sustained ground
combat are depleting military manpower and gear faster

than they can be replenished. Shortfalls of recruiting and
backlogs in needed equipment are taking a toll, and
growing numbers of units have been broken apart or
taxed by repeated deployments, particularly in the Army
National Guard and Reserves.[7]

This erosion, in turn, has led to a decline in the overall readiness of
U.S. ground forces to respond to threats domestically and internationally at a time when the United States has declared a global antiterrorism campaign that might last for generations. The nation also
saw in dramatic terms the need for the National Guard to respond
to Hurricane Katrina at a time when most National Guardsmen and
women were serving second and third tours in Iraq.

The need for the restoration of military units across the board,
with a substantial increase in personnel trained in military police and
civil affairs roles, provides an opportunity and a challenge for restructuring U.S. forces for a century of new kinds of conflicts. But even
this rebuilding and restructuring effort is now being hampered by
declining retention rates and increasing frustrations with recruitment.

If we are serious about our security shield and spear, our military
power must be adapted to counter new threats and take advantage of
new opportunities through the dramatic reform of military institutions
as well as their strategies, tactics, and doctrines. There must be rapid
shifts, however painful, in types of weapons and systems of weapons
procurement. The separate special operations forces of the services—
Rangers, Delta Force, SEALS, and special air force units—must be
further integrated and made cooperative across service barriers and
command structures. And, perhaps more important than everything
else, we must use our best innovative skills to transform human and
technological intelligence collection and analysis.

7. Ann Scott Tyson, "Two Years Later, Iraq War Drains Military," *Washington
Post*, March 19, 2005.

Intelligence Reform?

After a bitter political battle, in which the president among many others had to reverse course, the U.S. intelligence community is being restructured by law. From my own experience, this will not be easy and it will probably create more problems than it solves. The reasons trace to 1947, the passage of the National Security Act of that year, and the creation of the Central Intelligence Agency against much resistance from the new Department of Defense (formerly the War Department). Most intelligence during World War II was collected by the newly created Office of Strategic Services (OSS) and by the military. The OSS was the forerunner of the CIA. When the CIA was created, it was not given control over all intelligence budgets despite its top official having the title of director of central intelligence. The military insisted on keeping, and eventually greatly expanding, its intelligence capabilities. Soon, advanced technologies increased those capabilities dramatically, particularly in the form of overhead satellites and electronic collection, or communications intelligence (Comint). The National Security Agency (NSA) grew to very large proportions as the central collection and analysis point for communications collection and analysis. Soon the National Reconnaissance Office (NRO) was formed to manage the burgeoning satellite collection capabilities. Both of these very large organizations as well as a number of others less well known joined the growing Defense Intelligence Agency as wards of the Pentagon. Thus, two major fiefdoms struggled for central control of intelligence, the CIA and the Pentagon. In pure dollar terms, the Pentagon won hands down with roughly 80 percent of an intelligence budget that came to exceed $40 billion a year.

When the 9/11 commission recommended creation of an "intelligence czar" and a new layer of management to blanket the whole intelligence community, the president, secretary of Defense, many congressional leaders, and others opposed this notion. Sufficient political pressure mounted to require some action, however, and those in opposition relented. After much resistance from the Pentagon, continuing mostly behind the scenes even after the president's position publicly shifted, legislation requiring reorganization was enacted. A new director of national intelligence (DNI) and beginning staff of five hundred (undoubtedly to multiply exponentially) have been authorized with at least theoretical control over all intelligence operations and their budgets. The Pentagon was successful in protecting its hold on tactical, that is, battlefield intelligence. Over time, when the dust has settled and memories have faded, expect the thin line separating the tactical from the strategic to disappear like the Cheshire cat (leaving only its smile).

The CIA now becomes subordinate to the director of national intelligence. Even before the creation of the new regime, the CIA was being dismantled from the top down by its new director, former congressman Porter Goss, possibly as punishment for its failures on 9/11, possibly for providing support to the false notion of weapons of mass destruction in Iraq, but most probably because it refused to produce intelligence, valid or not, to justify further preemptive wars, for example, in Iran. Covert operations were being shifted from the CIA to murky new offices at the Pentagon with no legal authorization or accountability. Quite probably, at least under the current administration, the new DNI will work hand in glove with the Pentagon in the name of coordination but in fact in order to further reduce the chance of the kind of intelligence independent of ideology and political passion, originally intended from the CIA, from complicating further foreign military adventures.

None of this reorganization guarantees a qualitative improvement in intelligence collection or analysis. It might possibly improve the sharing of intelligence among various agencies to enable dots to be connected, but such intelligence will have to pass through yet another layer of management to do so and will still require the good will, conscientious dedication, and sense of the national interest of those who hold it, requirements for which no organizational solution exists. My background in all of these areas leads me to be skeptical of this reorganization's success as measured by discernible increases in the quality and coordination of intelligence. A great deal more money will be spent for the new layer of intelligence management with modest improvement in information sharing among intelligence agencies but without measurable improvement in the quality of intelligence gathered or without real resolution of traditional CIA-Pentagon antagonisms.

None of this struggle over bureaucratic turf mattered to the three thousand Americans killed on 9/11. It is doubtful that their last thoughts were of government bureaucracy and Washington power struggles. It is left to us surviving Americans to sort through the rubble made by those airplanes, not only of buildings but also of the intelligence services of the United States, and to see what can be done to guarantee that it never happens again. To do this, *superior intelligence must be guaranteed by making our intelligence services independent of political or ideological domination.*

Killing the Nearest Snake

Superior intelligence is useful only if it reveals dangers against which action can be taken. There is now an impending danger which cannot be avoided by massive intelligence reforms because we already know it exists. We simply choose not to do much about it. This danger is the theft or sale of ready-made nuclear weapons from the Russian (and perhaps other) arsenals. With the possible exception of a terrorist-inspired viral epidemic, a nuclear explosion or even a conventional explosion disseminating radioactive materials (a so-called dirty bomb) in a densely populated urban area—any one of dozens of cities—would cause mass casualties on a catastrophic scale both from the blast itself and from radioactive fallout. Yet current programs to secure such weapons, decommission them, and prevent others from being built, especially in Russia, are proceeding at the kind of leisurely pace that suggests no sense of urgency at all.

Along with others, Professor Graham Allison, former dean of the Kennedy School at Harvard, has documented this case in great detail, both the dangers represented by nuclear weapons in terrorists' hands and the lassitude of the U.S. government in preventing this catastrophe.[8] Almost everyone who has studied the issue concludes that this is the greatest danger America and its allies face today. Yet no one seems able to account for priorities that place the overthrow of Saddam Hussein, who did not have nuclear weapons, higher than prevention of the escape of such weapons, which are stockpiled in massive numbers in loosely guarded Russian arsenals.

A 2001 report concluded, "[T]he most urgent unmet national security threat to the United States today is the danger that weapons of mass destruction or weapons-usable material in Russia could be stolen and sold to terrorists or hostile nation-states and used against American troops abroad or citizens at home." Yet, over the past five years, the amount the United States is spending to address this threat has been going down. One expert called this "the single largest public policy failure in recent memory," and another called it the worst failure of [U.S.] government in modern times." James Fallows has written: "The single worst threat to America's future," loose nuclear weapons, "has the clearest solution," a program to lock up all fissionable material. But that solution is not being pursued.[9] This is the height of folly.

No one has suggested that the Russian government would be complicit in selling off these weapons or the technology required to make them, in the way the Pakistani government seemed to be with Abdul Q. Khan, simply because any of these nuclear weapons in the

8. Graham T. Allison, *Nuclear Terrorism: The Ultimate Preventable Catastrophe* (New York: Times Books, 2004).

9. James Fallows, "Success without Victory," *Atlantic Monthly*, January–February 2005.

hands of Chechnyan separatists could be and probably would be used against Russia itself before they would be used against the United States. This underscores the often overlooked fact that the United States is not the only target of terrorism in the world. Most experts believe that the real danger comes from grossly underpaid Russian nuclear scientists who possess nuclear weapons development knowledge or even more grossly underpaid young military guards at nuclear arsenals who possess the keys to the storage areas deciding, whether out of greed, malice, or coercion, to turn over either knowledge or keys for a lot of money.

Immediate protection can be achieved by urgently raising fences, broadening perimeters, training the protective services and paying them better, and tightening up security all the way around. Greater security also requires paying Russia's nuclear scientists a decent wage and giving them productive work to do in the peaceful uses of nuclear energy and in the dismantling of the nuclear arsenal. Long-term security requires decommissioning the bombs and warheads, an expensive, delicate, and highly technical undertaking requiring special facilities, highly skilled workers, and a process for safe disposal of the resulting highly radioactive nuclear wastes. All of this has been known since the end of the Cold War in 1991. Through the Nunn-Lugar Act, Congress took steps in the early 1990s to finance the systematic dismantling of the former Soviet nuclear arsenal. As difficult as it is to believe, funds for this program were cut in the first George W. Bush administration. A modest level of financing is finally being provided but without any demonstration of urgency by political leaders that comes close to matching the degree of danger this threat represents.

Examined from the broad perspective of security in the twenty-first century, there are few more urgent projects or projects that lend themselves more clearly to concrete, practical, immediate solution than reduction of vulnerable nuclear stockpiles. And none lend themselves more clearly to the notion that security is now a common, not an individual, undertaking. Like Russia, the United States has many more nuclear bombs and warheads than it could ever conceivably need. Unlike those in Russia, however, the American arsenals are highly and professionally protected (though there are periodic reports of simulated "attack teams" that penetrate the defenses with ease), and America's nuclear scientists are much less likely to sell off secrets or defect to al Qaeda out of financial desperation. We should focus on the Russian arsenal not because it is Russian but rather because it is redundant and vulnerable to penetration.

Given these widely accepted facts, and given the overall danger of weapons of mass destruction falling into terrorists' hands, it would seem axiomatic that all rational leaders would focus like a laser on this urgent problem. That is not happening. Even more perplexing, those responsible for making it happen have not been called to account for their laxity, inaction, and lack of urgency.

One might argue that the wars in Afghanistan and Iraq have preoccupied senior American officials. But this argument is not plausible. Wars must be fought on many fronts simultaneously. Faced with imminent threat, even dominant powers do not have the luxury of fighting one battle at a time. There is no inherent reason, barring pure obsession, why the invasion and occupation of Iraq, as absorbing as that has been, should prevent a great power from dismantling Russian nuclear arsenals at the same time. Different projects, different people. Expensive? Yes. But there cannot be a better or more productive investment in security at this moment than eliminating decaying nuclear stockpiles. Certainly, every dollar spent on this project will yield more immediate tangible security for the United States and the world than the hundreds of billions being spent in Iraq. Indeed, from a national security perspective, it was (and still is) a lot more important to destroy Russia's nuclear weapons than to invade Iraq.

If a pillar for a new security foundation were to be constructed from this analysis it might be this: *Address the most immediate threats first, and do not let long-term schemes distract from the actions required to produce immediate security.* Sometimes a security shield can be strengthened by proactive steps to eliminate risks.

Security through Diplomacy

America's security is America's concern. But America cannot achieve more than a modest degree of security without the help of friendly nations and without seeking to make friends of nations that have heretofore not been friendly. In both cases, diplomacy is required. Traditionally, Americans have been disdainful of diplomats. "Cookie pushers," they were often called by some backwoods members of Congress, who saw the diplomat as a necessary nuisance at best and a bumbling bureaucrat requiring rescue by marines at worst. Like it or not, no nation, including the United States, has found it possible to maintain relations with other nations without using those skilled in the complex arts of understanding and relating to strangers. Where America has suffered from its diplomats, it has almost always been from those not skilled in these arts yet who have been given high diplomatic appointments because of political contributions and a desire for the title of ambassador.

For anyone ignorant enough to ask regarding foreign nations, "Who cares?" the answer is simple: We need their help. We needed their help and they needed ours in two world wars and the Cold War. We promote "coalition forces" in Iraq even when they exist largely in the president's imagination. We need their help to track down terrorists, terrorist money, and terrorist weapons in their countries and in places where we cannot go. We need their help to control the spread of weapons of mass destruction. We need their help to finance our debt. We need their help to buy our products. We need their doctors and nurses when we run short of medical personnel. We need their help to regulate communications, sea lanes, and epidemics and to pursue an endless agenda of common concerns. If the price we pay for all of this and more is to push a cookie or two, so be it.

But, say the go-it-aloners, the international organizations we are involved in do not work well. There is much to this, and there are two reasons for it: One is that, in the case of the United Nations particularly, they were created in a different time for different purposes than they are now called on to confront; and the other is that we ourselves have often purposely structured them so that they do not work too well. Most of the world organizations with which we are most familiar date to the mid-twentieth century and the period between World War II and the beginning of the Cold War. These include the United Nations itself, the World Bank and International Monetary Fund, the North Atlantic Treaty Organization, and a host of others. Many of them were constructed either to prevent another world war or to help contain communism or both. On any scale of effectiveness, they have succeeded. There has not been another world war, and communism has been severely contained. Additionally, the issue of national sovereignty, the right of every nation to control its own internal affairs, caused us to insist on preserving our right to do things our own way when we chose to rather than to give these institutions the kind of power necessary to make them even more effective.

Are diplomacy and international organizations necessary to achieve security in the twenty-first century? Absolutely. The British diplomat Robert Cooper believes that the increasingly interdependent, postmodern Europe has virtually eliminated war within its territory and that territory is expanding to bring in new members in Eastern Europe as well, possibly, as the Balkans and Turkey at the gates of the Muslim world. But he correctly points out that the price of peace and integration is national sovereignty: "Making peace is as much part of sovereignty as making war. For the postmodern state sovereignty is a seat at the table."[10] Leaving traditional politics and conventional diplomacy aside, a twenty-first-century security cloak requires much greater regional and international integration, which itself will require substantial reexamination

10. Robert Cooper, *The Breaking of Nations: Order and Chaos in the Twenty-First Century* (New York: Atlantic Monthly Press, 2003).

of the nature of national sovereignty. If the table is where security is negotiated and achieved, and if the price of a seat at the table is some degree of national sovereignty, that is a price it would be foolish not to pay.

A number of examples suggest themselves. The first, biological warfare, has been mentioned. Recently, scientists have announced breakthroughs in the ability to synthesize large viruses including, for example, smallpox. The implications of this capability for terrorism's threat are staggering. Further, given modern mass air transportation, the ability of evil-doers to disseminate viruses, smallpox or others, is virtually limitless. Suicidal terrorists themselves can be the carriers and thus become human plague bombs. To believe that any nation, including the biggest target of all, the United States, can defeat this threat by itself is the height of folly. Experts have argued that we now have no choice but to mobilize international skills, experts, and laboratories and to integrate public health and national security communities across borders to develop vaccine stockpiles and rapid response capabilities to isolate and quarantine infected victims and massively inoculate those as yet uninfected.

If these steps toward international cooperation and integration are begun before, not after, the threat is activated, experts offer some good news:

> If the trans-Atlantic community regarded biological
> weapons and the deliberate epidemics they would bring
> as one of the most grave and urgent challenges to
> international security—and if we were to respond with
> the level of resources and intellectual firepower that the
> free world brought to the defeating [of] Communism—
> then we could, in our generation, eliminate bioweapons
> as agents of mass lethality.[11]

11. Daniel Hoffman and Tara O'Toole, "Facing Up to the Bioterror Threat," *International Herald Tribune*, January 31, 2005.

There is that word *urgent* popping up again. For inexplicable reasons, the urgency lacking in dismantling the Russian nuclear arsenal is also lacking in organizing our friends and allies against the equally manageable biological threat.

Of the many areas where increased cooperation across national boundaries is required, perhaps the most important is peace making. Since the end of the Cold War, the United States has been the world's default peace maker. The phrase *peace making* is used here in its literal sense: stopping violence, if necessary with force. From biblical times, "blessed are the peace makers." Everywhere possible, peace should be made through peaceful means: negotiation, arbitration, and diplomacy. In an age where tribal violence can become national violence and national violence can become international violence, leaving violence unattended invites catastrophe not only for the victims—as in Rwanda, Kosovo, and Darfur—but also for the wider world. (It is a commonplace to cite the assassination of Archduke Ferdinand as the trigger for World War I.) Occasionally, however, diplomacy does not work, and force is required. A large Colt revolver popular among sheriffs on the American frontier was called the Peacemaker.

Blessed Are the Peace Makers

The question for Americans is: Do we really want to be the world's peace maker? Most Americans would say, "No. Let's let others do it or at least get their help." Based on my own long-held concern for security issues and observing the post–Cold War trend to let the Americans carry the load, I have urged for some time that we take the lead in organizing an international peace-*making* force, a permanent, standing coalition of the willing. That force's task would be what its name suggests, to halt violence, particularly genocidal violence that could, by spreading, endanger regional or international stability.

Our present policy is either to handle the problem ourselves at the cost of our own lives and money, or to do nothing, or to take the time required to construct ad hoc coalitions of the willing, time often used by evil-doers to slaughter tens of thousands of innocent people. Instead of relying on these flawed policies, we should form a standing force on a permanent basis in anticipation of future violence. The reason this has not been done to date is the same one that has limited the effectiveness of international organizations in the past: national sovereignty. The brave Canadian general commanding U.N. peace-keeping forces in Rwanda, General Roméo Dallaire, has stated that, given early U.N. authorization, approximately 900 troops might have prevented the slaughter of 800,000 Tutsis by Hutus from even beginning, but that even after the mass killings were under way, fewer than 5,000 troops, which no nation including the United States would send, could have ended the slaughter and saved hundreds of thousands of Tutsi lives.[12]

The question is whether it is better to do nothing, go it alone, or cobble together ad hoc coalitions on the one hand, or to create an international constabulary force on the other hand, a force with at least a limited capability to stop violence and set the table for the peace keepers and diplomats. As with suppressing bioterror and a host of other twenty-first-century security issues, *going it together will beat going it alone every time.*

All of this suggests ways in which the United States might make its powers and resources more relevant in an age of new threats and new opportunities and in an age of a more complex security chess board. Obviously, this is a wide-ranging challenge that must take into account a series of realities: To ensure continuing public support, we should pursue security policies honestly and openly with the Ameri-

12. "Leave None to Tell the Story: Genocide in Rwanda," report of Human Rights Watch, March 1999.

can people; we must reform our thinking on defense priorities and military structures; further erosion of civic membership will destroy the social cohesion necessary for a secure nation; substantial increases in investment in education in the sciences and technology are crucial for American strength and leadership; to finance our security, we must replace debt and consumption with investment and productivity; to achieve superior intelligence, our intelligence services must be free from political ideologies; the most immediate security threats, such as Russian nuclear arsenals and bioterrorism, must be addressed first and urgently; and going it together in peace making is a much greater guarantee of security than going it alone.

The Security of the Commons

V

Overview and Objectives

America's great task in the twenty-first century is to create a new commonwealth of security, one that comprehends the complicated global chess board and incorporates the notion of a security shield and a security cloak.

In the past, in wars against fascism, imperialism, and communism, we gained security through larger armies and navies, advanced weapons systems, and deployment of our powerful armed forces abroad. These steps enabled us to keep insecurity at a safe distance. For a time, we were not interested in insecurity. But insecurity was interested in us. Now insecurity has shredded national boundaries, leapfrogged great armies, and is all around us. The threats to our security are new, and many of these threats resist traditional military solutions. In many ways, the combined solutions are interrelated. A healthy economy is necessary to provide security of livelihood. A strong dollar and greater independence from foreign creditors are necessary for our economic security. A healthy environment is necessary to provide security for future generations. Dependable energy supplies that do not require the continued loss of American lives are necessary to our economic and social security. A world-class education system is crucial to American leadership and security.

Terrorism is not a belief system nor an ideology espoused by a nation that can be defeated in conventional combat. It is a method of coercion that cannot be defeated by traditional military means. It can only be confined by anticipating the actions of those who employ this method, restricting their opportunities, penetrating their organizations, denying them financial resources, impeding their recruitment, interdicting their weapons, totally denying them access to weapons of mass destruction, pursuing and destroying their leadership faster than it can be replaced, and most of all being quicker and smarter. Welcome to the new security chess game of the twenty-first century.

Imagine terrorism to be the fear created in a garden by the presence of a lethal plant that spreads its seeds widely and strangles all other plants. The fear it creates cannot be eliminated either by fencing the predator plant off nor by running a bulldozer through the garden. This plant must be denied sunlight, water, and fertilizer; it must be prevented from sprouting; and it must be pulled up by the roots. In many ways, creating a shield against it sprouting and spreading its seeds is the most effective method of preventing this lethal plant from threatening the garden.

By virtue of globalization and information, the United States is now firmly embedded in an international commons. Traditionally, the commons was a space belonging to all which could be used and enjoyed by all. No one owned it because everyone owned it. *Security in the twenty-first century must be considered a virtual commons, because security both as shield and cloak has become indivisible.* My insecurity makes you insecure, and your insecurity makes me insecure. In many ways, the traditional language relating to national security will mean less and less. It will be increasingly difficult, perhaps even impossible, to achieve national security in an insecure world. National security is at best relative and at worst obsolete.

From classic times, so powerfully resonant with our founders, the Greek city-state conducted the republic's business in the *ecclesia*, the assembly for citizens and citizen-soldiers; and in the Roman republic, the Campus Martius was the site for meetings of the assembly of Roman citizens, who would gather to discuss the interests of the commonwealth. From the ideal of the commonwealth, the essence of the republic, was the notion of the commons born and with it the sense that all citizens of the republic had a stake in their common security. The security of the United States in the twenty-first century will require restoration of this republican ideal.

The diplomat Robert Cooper has appropriately written that nations have traditionally had three instruments for dealing with the world: diplomacy, finance, and the military or, put more bluntly: persuasion, bribery, and coercion. America's security in the twenty-first century will depend on its ability to use persuasion, with bribery where required, to enlarge the commons so that the necessity of coercion will diminish, and when it does become necessary, it will be collective. The security of the twenty-first-century commons will be collaborative, proactive, multidimensional, and civic: collaborative because it will be in everyone's interest to enforce the written and unwritten laws on acceptable human behavior; proactive because a bomb deactivated is an explosion never felt; multidimensional because security has economic, social, and political, as well as military, components; and civic because membership in the commons requires some degree of contribution, participation, and sense of duty.

What principles should we use in establishing this new republic of security? First, *our economic cloak is the basis of our strength, and our strength is the basis for our world leadership.* American leadership will depend on three major policies: investment in education, science, technology, and innovation; energy security; and increased productivity.

Second, *America's role in the world is to resist hegemony without seeking hegemony by the creation of a new global commonwealth focused on stability, growth, and security.* America's new role in the world will require several policy innovations: the reform of existing international institutions or the creation of new ones adapted to the new realities of this century; aggressive development programs involving micro-lending; urgent control of the proliferation of weapons of mass destruction and the destruction of existing arsenals; and the creation of a new international peace-making force.

Third, *to respond to the century's new threats, the U.S. military shield must be composed of these principles: flexibility, reform, and intelligence.* Several policies form the centerpiece of today's military security: an appreciation of fourth-generation warfare; military reform principles applied to strength and numbers of personnel, strategy, tactics, doctrine, and weapons procurement; creation of a fifth military service composed of combined special forces; and the development of a new human intelligence corps.

Economic Transformation

The security of Americans requires economic opportunity and prosperity. America's leadership in this century is directly dependent on its economic vitality. We may well try to combine the largest military in the world with a stagnant economy, but this will not succeed for long. An economy that can produce only weapons is not an economy that can support its people, provide economic energy for others, or even eventually maintain its military strength. Other nations observe whether we are creative, innovative, and dynamic. If we are not demonstrating these characteristics relative to other thriving nations, the United States will lose its position of leadership and our ability to influence the direction of like-minded societies.

There are many current indicators that all is well, that we can continue neglecting knowledge, energy security, and productivity and still continue our life style. Why transform our economic base, conventional thinking asks, when we can continue to rely on attracting foreign scientists, pay whatever price foreign oil producers demand, and borrow from foreigners to sustain our materialistic values?

Since we are in an increasingly interdependent world, it might be asked, what is wrong with this kind of reliance on foreigners for knowledge, oil, and credit? After all, don't they rely on us for hamburgers, coffee, rock music, and bad movies? Those who find this a fair exchange are welcome to their delusions. Our age, being entranced with doctrines of laissez faire and market capitalism, does not permit either the notion that the difference between the foundations of our economy and its window dressings is huge or the suggestion that government has a central role to play in maintaining and improving our economy's foundation through active public policies.

In almost every age of expansion, our nation's government took steps to empower commerce and industry. In the nineteenth century, these steps included acquiring lands to the Pacific Ocean; granting rights across it to railroad builders; patenting land to homesteaders; making mineral deposits available to prospectors for a pittance (a policy that still survives); building roads, highways, and waterways for commerce; establishing land-grant colleges; and a host of similar public goods and social investments.

In the twentieth century, the pattern continued with farm subsidies; the privatization of military research that developed the jet engine and other inventions, such as the Internet; creating whole industries; the G.I. Bill of Rights; medical research benefiting the pharmaceutical industry; interstate highway systems; scholarship programs for mass higher education; the national laboratory system; space exploration; the creation of the nuclear power industry; and an amazing variety of other subsidies for private enterprises. In some

THE SHIELD AND THE CLOAK

countries, private industries fear a take-over by the government. In America, we might well fear the reverse.

This is not a polemic for government or against the private sector. It is a reminder that periods of national expansion have almost always been dependent on major stimulative actions taken by the nation's government. The private sector will not close the gap now growing between America's current educational performance and the knowledge base we must have. Private industry will not, on its own, make America energy secure. The private sector cannot, even if it wanted to, reverse the low savings rate and high debt ratio in the United States.

Markets can do many wondrous and mysterious things. Defining and protecting the national interest is not one. The profit motive does not necessarily guarantee national or individual security. Unless the government of the United States begins to take urgent steps to reverse these structural vulnerabilities, America will become increasingly insecure. And that insecurity will not be caused by terrorism or competing nations.

To establish the republic of security, the first step is to invest in creative knowledge as a national objective.

The Centrality of Knowledge

"Second only to a weapon of mass destruction detonating in an American city," forecast the U.S. Commission on National Security/ 21st Century in January 2001, "we can think of nothing more dangerous than a failure to manage properly science, technology, and education for the common good over the next quarter century."[1] These are strong words, strongly felt, and very worth repeating.

In the twenty-first century, the engines of economic growth will be science and technology. The United States is not produc-

1. *Road Map for National Security: Imperative for Change*, final report of the U.S. Commission on National Security/21st Century, Washington, D.C., January 31, 2001, p. 29.

ing enough scientists, mathematicians, physicists, and engineers or those qualified to teach in these fields at the public school, university, or graduate school levels. Much of the research that created the basis for U.S. security in the Cold War era was produced in the national laboratory system. Since the end of the Cold War, that system has been in decline. Other nations in Europe and Asia, especially the Chinese, are increasing their investment in all fields of science and in scientific and technological research.

There is a lag time in all scientific fields between the time that a scientist is educated, that scientist begins her research, her research is tested and proved, her proved research is applied to production, her product reaches the arsenals of our defenders or the shelves of commercial markets, and the full economic impact of that research and production is felt. A scholarship to that young science student may not pay dividends for years, but those dividends may be realized for decades and may have ripple effects even longer. Scientific and technological knowledge are the seed corn of the United States' future growth and prosperity. It must be accumulated and sown on an urgent basis.

In January 2001, the commission recommended doubling the U.S. government's research and development budget by 2010 and instituting a more competitive environment for the allocation of those funds. It also recommended elevating the responsibilities of the president's science advisor, resuscitation of the national laboratory system, and further recommended a new national security science and technology education act to produce a dramatic increase in the number of science and engineering professionals and qualified teachers in science and math. A quarter of a million new science and mathematics teachers are needed in America's public schools in this decade.[2] Much of this thinking mirrored the transformation in science and technology brought on by the dramatically increased U.S.

2. *Road Map for National Security: Imperative for Change*, final report of the U.S. Commission on National Security/21st Century, Washington, D.C., January 31, 2001, p. xiv.

investment stimulated by the Soviet launch of its Sputnik satellite in the 1950s. None of these things has been done or has even been begun.

Rather than invade Middle Eastern countries whose possession of weapons of mass destruction or whose threat to the United States is at best dubious, we should cultivate our greatest national resource, the human mind. We should encourage it in directions that will strengthen our nation by stimulating economic growth and reward it for pursuing the objectives required to keep our nation on science's and technology's cutting edges. The specific fields of most promise for economic growth are information technologies, biotechnology, environmental research, nanotechnologies, and, perhaps most important, breakthrough energy technologies. There are direct and demonstrable linkages between a knowledge base and a well-educated work force, between a well-educated work force and productivity, between productivity and national prosperity, between prosperity and national cohesion, and between national cohesion and national security.

Energy Invulnerability

America's security requires two additional major steps: dramatic changes in our energy consumption patterns and the creation of a zone of international interest in the Persian Gulf.

So long as the economy of the United States is held hostage by foreign oil producers, America will remain vulnerable to price rises, the interruption of oil supplies by terrorists, the overthrow of producing governments, and regional unrest, instability, and conflict. In just over a decade, America has fought two wars, one still under way, in the most unstable region of the world, the Persian Gulf. Oil imports are the leading factor in our massive and growing trade deficits. Some of the money we send to oil producers finds its way into the hands of terrorists. We are thus helping to finance our own destruction.

The economy of the United States cannot be fully transformed and American security reclaimed without a planned commitment to become sufficiently independent of vulnerable foreign oil supplies so that their probable, possibly inevitable, interruption does not cause major economic dislocation or require American military forces to sacrifice themselves in large numbers to recapture those supplies.

Our national goal does not have to be zero imports or absolute independence from foreign oil supplies. Our goal should be to achieve, as quickly as possible, a sufficient degree of independence from foreign supplies that interruption of those supplies does not require us to go to war. Some foreign oil supplies are more stable than others. As a general proposition, Western Hemisphere sources, such as Mexico and Venezuela (the former more than the latter), are more dependable than suppliers elsewhere. In general also, supplies from elsewhere, including Russia, are more stable than those from the Persian Gulf. And finally, some smaller producers in the Persian Gulf are more stable then others, including Saudi Arabia. Thus it is possible to rank foreign oil sources by relative degrees of vulnerability and to begin the process of shifting imports away from those with the highest degree of risk to those with lower degrees of risk.

Additional steps must be taken. There is tremendous waste in U.S. energy consumption. Most of this waste occurs in the transportation sector, and most of this sector's waste is represented by the automobile. We drive wasteful cars. Everyone knows, but too few wish to acknowledge, that fuel efficiency improvements in passenger vehicles would save massive amounts of energy—and money. The issue is not one of knowledge; the issue is one of the political will of the society and the personal will of individual citizens.

The president and most members of Congress do not want to tell their constituents that they will pay a penalty if they do not buy and drive smaller, lighter, cleaner, and more-efficient vehicles. If they had the courage to do so, we could begin immediately to reverse our energy insecurity. The most effective way to demonstrate this courage would be to admit this central fact: *America's energy policy is to continue to depend on foreign oil supplies so that we can drive big, wasteful vehicles and, if those supplies are cut off, to sacrifice the lives of our sons and daughters to get the oil.*

Iraq violated international law by invading Kuwait and deserved to be forced to withdraw. But few will admit that Gulf War I was more about oil than democracy (Kuwait then and now not being a democratic country) and that oil played at least some role in the decision to launch Gulf War II. Any policy that we are ashamed to admit is probably not an honorable policy. Confronted with these facts, defenders of our two Gulf wars claim that, even if we were energy secure, we have a duty to keep oil supplies flowing to other consumers in Europe and Asia. They are correct to point out that many of our allies are proportionately more dependent on imported oil than we are and that interruption of their energy supplies would disrupt world markets, including ours.

The political issue is this: Should the United States necessarily assume the responsibility to guarantee the rest of the world's oil supplies? Why not, say the conventional thinkers, we have the biggest army, we spend more on our military, and we are the greatest power in the world. This is our job, they say. If so, this should be explained forthrightly to the American people in a way that no president to date has done. Where the lives of American forces are at stake, the American people have a right to know that we are the world's de facto oil cops, and our leaders have a duty to tell us.

This is the reasoning behind the constitutional requirement that only Congress, the representatives of the people, not the president, can declare war, despite the almost total abdication of congressional responsibility for declaring war since World War II. No American president has ever stated that America will guarantee the rest of the world's oil supplies, nor has any president asked Congress for authority to do so. But that seems to be our unstated, if not secret, policy.

Here, our energy policy has close parallels to our preemptive policy in Iraq. In both cases, the true reasons for our actions were not candidly disclosed to the American people. In both cases, the reasons for this resistance to candor are the same. Our leaders doubted that we would endorse their actions if we were told the truth. It is not an implausible policy to invade Iraq, depose Saddam Hussein, and use that country as our political and military base in the wider Middle East. It is not an implausible policy to assume unilateral responsibility for guaranteeing a flow of oil from that region to the rest of the world. In both cases, however, to tell the truth about the reasons for our actions is to acknowledge a reality that our leaders wish to keep hidden: *These are acts of empire*—an attempt to impose our will on other nations by force—not acts of a republic legitimately seeking its own security.

Where the conduct of nations is concerned, the historian Barbara Tuchman defined folly as the conscious pursuit of a flawed policy knowing that a more plausible alternative exists. There are more plausible alternatives in the Persian Gulf. The United States should propose that the United Nations declare the Persian Gulf region to be a zone of international interest and under that designation seek authorization to create a peace-keeping body composed of international forces, including particularly forces from nations dependent on the region's oil, to guarantee the free flow of oil from the region. This protective force would be trained to resist terrorist attacks or the interference of any nation or collection of nations from within or from outside the region with the transportation of oil from any producing country. Special protection would be given to refineries, tanker terminals, and sea-lane straits and choke points.

This notion is not totally without international precedent. The Antarctic Treaty (1959) ensuring the use of Antarctica for peaceful purposes only, the Outer Space Treaty (1967) making the exploration and use of outer space the province of all of humanity, the Law of the Sea Convention (1982) seeking to reserve the high seas for peaceful purposes (but failing ratification), and the Moon Agreement (1979) prohibiting the militarization of the moon and other celestial bodies—all suggest sufficient international interest in areas and resources, terrestrial and extraterrestrial, to make special provisions to protect, demilitarize, and provide common administration for them. Areas set aside for special protection from conflict in the past have most often been called either international zones of peace or zones of peace and cooperation.[3] In none of these cases of international treaty making is a special enforcement mechanism, of the sort I suggest with the Persian Gulf zone of international interest, provided. Rather, these precedents rely on international law and international tribunals to guarantee their enforcement.

For reasons of international law, the special Persian Gulf force proposed here most probably could not be given authority to interfere in the internal politics of any nation. Challenging questions arise in this arena in any case, even if no enforcement provision is included. But critics must answer at least this question: What will the United States do unilaterally, in its present capacity as the self-appointed ad hoc guarantor of world oil supplies, if an internal coup overthrows the Saudi royal family? Unquestionably, we have contingency plans to intervene in Saudi Arabia under those conditions, whether to put the Saudi royals back into power or to substitute our own hand-picked successor (a Saudi Chalabi, more or less), whatever the prospect for success. Whether such plans would be enacted under those circumstances is left to speculation.

In either case, however, whether outside interference or internal upheaval, the presence of a U.N.-sanctioned international force

3. See Arthur H. Westing, ed., *Global Resources and International Conflict: Environmental Factors in Strategic Policy and Action* (Oxford: Oxford University Press, 1986); Surya P. Sudedi, *Land and Maritime Zones of Peace in International Law* (Oxford: Clarendon, 1996); and Christopher C. Joyner and Sudhir K. Chopra, eds., *The Antarctic Legal Regime* (Boston: Martinus Nijhoff, 1988). I am indebted to Professor Vaughan Lowe, All Souls College, Oxford, for these authoritative references.

prepared, trained, equipped, and authorized to prevent a global economic domino effect would be a vastly superior political and military option to that of the United States acting alone. Another variation on this theme might be the creation of a Persian Gulf Treaty Alliance (PGTA), patterned after the North Atlantic Treaty Alliance (NATO), an alliance in this case composed of both oil producers and oil consumers. Such an alliance would agree that all parties engaged in it would collectively guarantee the flow of oil from the region's producers to global consumers. In contrast with NATO, which was a security alliance formed to guarantee the integrity of Western Europe against any threat of Soviet expansion or coercion, the Persian Gulf Treaty Alliance would be resource based and would ensure the flow of oil necessary to maintain a growing world economy.

This central fact remains: So long as the United States relies on unstable oil supplies to the degree that its economic well-being is held hostage, we will not be secure. A domestic plan for energy security based on a reduction of dependence on unstable foreign oil supplies, conservation, energy efficient transportation including fuel-efficiency standards and hybrid cars, development of alternative and renewable resources, sulfur-free coal gasification (using integrated, combined-cycle technologies), acceleration of hydrogen technologies, and other readily available steps, together with an internationally sanctioned plan for protecting Persian Gulf exports, whether a zone of international interest or a PGTA, would restore a much greater degree of security to the U.S. economy and relieve the United States of continuing to be the principal or only guarantor of the security of oil supplies.

Security through Productivity

To be truly serious about achieving security, we must reverse our national priorities and values. The simplest way to do this is to reward production and to tax consumption. Currently, to put it as directly as possible, we are consuming more than we produce and borrowing to finance the difference. Individuals who do this soon find themselves in bankruptcy. Even seemingly wealthy nations such as the United States cannot continue to do so forever.

Though not easy, the alternative is simple. Reward savings, investment, and productivity, principally through the tax code, and likewise penalize borrowing, debt, and consumption. How might this work? All income saved and productively invested, including in savings accounts, would be taxed only upon its reclamation and expenditure. All other income would be progressively taxed. This is vastly different from so-called supply-side arguments fashionable in the 1980s and beyond in one important degree: The supply-side argument cuts taxes in the *hope* that income will be saved and invested; this idea *requires* income to be saved and invested before receiving the tax reward. Though many refinements are available, this is the core idea.

But what of the United States itself? If it were to fundamentally alter its treatment of privately earned income, should it not also tighten its belt? At the very least, our government should not provide massive tax cuts when entering a war. To do so, as the current administration did before invading Iraq, is to suggest that a policy of war offers its own financial rewards and that, in any case, the costs of war can be deferred or never paid. Most important, it severs the costs of the war from the decision to go to war and thus requires no citizen calculation on whether a purely voluntary war is worth waging.

Clearly, the greatest cost of war is human life, the lives of our young sons and daughters and those innocent civilians in the nation we target. But a distant yet important second calculation is based on the pocketbook. Even to suggest that we do not have to pay for waging war is both cynical and immoral.

If one of the several reasons for waging war in oil-rich regions has to do with our dependency on that oil, then we could achieve the twin aims of reducing budget deficits and encouraging energy independence by taxing oil imports on a graduated scale and taxing its principal inefficient uses: propelling large, heavy vehicles. Taxes on wasteful and unnecessary consumption are taxes on luxury, in this case, the luxury of driving a big car when someone else's son may have to die in order for you to enjoy that luxury. The issue about valuing productivity over consumption is not simply an issue of taxation or even energy use; it is a genuine issue of values. It also is central to the issue of individual and national security.

To be a debtor nation, to rely on others for credit, is to be an insecure nation. It is now generally agreed, perhaps since President Richard Nixon declared himself and others "Keynesians," that tax cutting or increased government spending are legitimate fiscal tools when a nation is in recession or depression. These are not legitimate tools to use in pursuing a hidden ideological agenda. It is one thing to cut taxes to stimulate job growth in order to cure unemployment; it is quite another thing to encourage tax cut after tax cut, targeted especially in favor of those with the greatest income, in order to incur such monstrous public deficits that worthwhile humanitarian public programs are required to be sacrificed.

With honest fiscal policies openly revealed, based on rewards for savings and investment and penalties for debt and consumption, the United States will quickly amass the capital required to finance new innovations, new technologies, new scientific and technological experimentation, new laboratories to explore biomedical breakthroughs to cure diseases, institutes to develop nanotechnologies, space projects designed for intelligence collection and global tracking of weapons of mass destruction, invention of renewable sources of energy, and thousands of projects capable of benefiting all of humanity and expanding opportunities for Americans and millions of others.

The nexus between energy dependence and debt, and among foreign policy, energy dependence, and debt, and the benefits of a policy of energy conservation and independence were cogently and accurately summarized by Thomas Friedman as follows:

> It would buy reform in some of the worst regimes in the world, from Tehran to Moscow [by reducing oil revenues]. It would reduce the chances that the U.S. and China are going to have a global struggle over oil—which is where we are heading. It would help us to strengthen the dollar and reduce the current accounts deficit by importing less crude. It would reduce climate change more than anything in Kyoto [Treaty]. It would significantly improve America's standing in the world by making us good global citizens. It would shrink the budget deficit. It would reduce our dependence on the Saudis so we could tell them the truth. (Addicts never tell the truth to their pushers.) And it would pull China away from its drift into supporting some of the worst governments in the world, like Sudan's, because it needs their oil. Most important, making energy independence our generation's moon shot could inspire more young people to go into science and engineering, which we desperately need.[4]

The more one looks at the realities of the twenty-first century, and the threats and opportunities these realities provide, the more one is drawn to the conclusion that they are almost all inextricably intertwined. Terrorism is a threat to U.S. national security. But on a different scale and in different dimensions, a stagnating education system, energy dependence, and debt-financed consumption are equal threats to our security. There are no military solutions to any of these foundational threats. Terrorists represent external threats

---

4. Thomas L. Friedman, "No Mullah Left Behind," *New York Times*, February 13, 2005.

which can be identified and destroyed. Ignorance, dependence, and materialism are more sinister and more dangerous because they represent cancers that have already invaded the body of our nation. They can be defeated, but only by a collective act of national will and truly strong, *honest* national leaders.

A new national security strategy of the shield and the cloak requires the transformation of our economy, transformation from declining educational investment to the creation of the best education system in the world, transformation from energy dependence to energy security, and transformation from consumption to production. These projects represent the core of a program of national renewal designed to improve America's security dramatically in the twenty-first century.

America's Role in the World: Resisting Hegemony without Seeking Hegemony

To achieve security, the United States must more clearly define its role in the world. From 1947 through 1991, our mission was the containment of communism. Since 9/11, it has been the war on terrorism. This is a necessary but not sufficient role for America to play. Our future security requires us to expand our leadership mission and define our broader objectives more clearly and coherently and with a greater sense of our own history, the revolutionary times in which we live, and the resources at our disposal. The discipline required to define our objectives demands that we think more clearly about ourselves and explain ourselves more clearly to the nations of the world.

At critical junctures in the history of the United States, we have undertaken to define what role we wished to play in global affairs. This was certainly true when President James Monroe and his secretary of State, John Quincy Adams, devised the Principles of 1823, years later called the Monroe Doctrine. These principles declared that Europe's efforts to colonize the Americas should cease and that, in return, the United States would disclaim any interest in participating on anyone's behalf in Europe's seemingly endless quarrels. Later in that century, President William McKinley used the occasion of the Spanish-American War to experiment with America as a colonial power replacing Spain in the Caribbean and the Philippines. Woodrow Wilson used the bloodletting of World War I as the occasion to promote the League of Nations and the notion of making the world, albeit peacefully and internationally, safe for democracy. Following World War II, President Harry Truman defined the role of the United States as the containment of communism. Since the collapse of the Soviet empire, the only specific mission declared by the United States is to fight terrorism and, more vaguely, to spread democracy.

In the pursuit of security through war on terrorism, our current government has undertaken a radical rewriting of the Monroe Doctrine. Rather than protecting the Western Hemisphere from European colonization, it has substituted a unilateral right to use preemptive and preventive invasions of any nation in the world that it deems might conceivably, at some undetermined time in the future, represent a threat to American interests. And, whereas James Monroe could make his principles against colonization credible because of an alliance with the British, the Bush doctrine is unilateralist, using U.S. military superiority as a substitute for both diplomacy and alliance. James Monroe would be amazed, and his successor in the White House, John Quincy Adams, would be appalled. For it was Adams who famously stated:

> America does not go abroad in search of monsters to
> destroy. She is the well-wisher to the freedom and
> independence of all. She is the champion only of her
> own. She will recommend the general cause by the

countenance of her voice, and the benignant [*sic*] sympathy of her example. She well knows that by once enlisting under other banners than her own, were they even the banners of foreign independence, she would involve herself beyond the powers of extrication, in all the wars of interest and intrigue, of individual avarice, envy, and ambition, which assumed the colors and usurped the standards of freedom. . . . She might become the dictatress of the world. She would be no longer ruler of her own spirit.[5]

Adams's precognition of Iraq, and possibly elsewhere, is both eerie and exact. But perhaps he understood the American character and purpose better than do those in power today.

Let us consider a more comprehensive role, one more in keeping with Adams's understanding of America: *The United States, in cooperation with other peaceful and democratic nations, will reform existing international institutions to make them more relevant to our times; where necessary we will propose new global institutions and networks to address new challenges; we will cooperatively explore new approaches to development in less-developed regions; we will structure coalitions to shrink the arsenals of weapons of mass destruction and to control technologies that threaten to expand them; and we will establish the means for collective enforcement of the peace.*

Support for International Institutions

In December 2004, the U.N. High Level Panel on Threats, Challenges, and Change reported its recommendations for restructuring the United Nations, especially its Security Council, and adapting its

5. Samuel Flagg Bemis, *John Quincy Adams and the Foundations of American Foreign Policy* (New York: Knopf, 1949), p. 356f.

role and missions. Following that report, U.N. secretary-general Kofi Annan recommended streamlining the General Assembly's deliberative processes, expanding the Security Council, replacing the Commission on Human Rights, and restructuring the Secretariat. Steps such as these are long overdue. Various reviews of the World Bank, of NATO, and of other political, economic, and security organizations have taken place from time to time. But the kind of dramatic and comprehensive, even Olympian, overview of all of these institutions that the twenty-first century requires has yet to take place.

The United Nations' peace-keeping authority is vague, contingent, and erratic. Its role in countering terrorism is uncertain and undefined. Its humanitarian missions, representing perhaps its greatest achievements to date, are uneven and now riddled with charges of impropriety. Its relationship with its most powerful member and founder, the United States, waxes and wanes, mostly due to fluctuations in U.S. politics.

Likewise, NATO, constituted to protect Western Europe from Soviet intimidation or encroachment, now seems to be an unfocused entity. Should it take a more aggressive role in preventing state failure and ethnic violence, as in Bosnia and Kosovo, in areas on its boundaries? Should it expand its membership to nations beyond Europe? Should it assume a greater global peace-making and peace-keeping role? Should it become the lead force in countering terrorism? Is NATO to be made redundant by a proposed European Union security force? Equally important, do we now need a whole new range of global or regional organizations to perform new missions?

All these questions require an affirmative answer. Times change; institutions must change. "We might as well require a man to wear still the coat which fitted him when a boy," said Thomas Jefferson, "as civilized societies to remain ever under the regimen of their barbarous ancestors." It is unrealistic to expect the laws and institutions of any period to adapt themselves to new realities and changing times, he continued, "laws and institutions must go hand in hand with the progress of the human mind."

In its own national security interest and to achieve the individual security of its citizens, the United States should exhibit the same degree of creativity in the early twenty-first century that it did in the vital transition period between the end of World War II and the beginning of the Cold War. The United Nations was created to prevent World War III, and it helped to do that. The North Atlantic Treaty Organization was created to contain communism, and it helped to do that.

Now, states need to be protected from failure; the increasingly interwoven international banking structure needs protection from collapse; the global environment requires global protection; weapons of mass destruction require international containment; epidemics and bioterrorism demand global cooperation for prevention; poor countries need concrete prospects of development opportunities to prevent mass migrations from south to north; and a host of new problems representing the third dimension on the security chess board requires new cooperative solutions and the means to implement them.

It is beyond the scope of a work such as this to define with any precision how a new generation of international cooperative institutions should look, how they should be structured, what their writs should be, or how they should carry out their functions. However, given the perils created by a conjunction of technology, weapons of mass destruction, and radical religious fundamentalism, new security threats require new capabilities and resources for their containment and eradication.

Given the increased ease that modern mass air transportation provides for the spread of contagious diseases, new mechanisms for containing, suppressing, and where possible eradicating such diseases are required.

Given the cumulative impact that widespread industrialization is now having on the global environment, the uneven actions of individual states are inadequate.

Given the globalization of finance and the massive amounts of capital flowing daily through a bewildering system of national banking systems, financial stability requires new international banking regulatory regimes.

Given the degree to which local violence can spread like wildfire, new international capabilities for suppression of that violence are required.

The number of twenty-first-century threats to security is growing. They all have one thing in common: No single nation, including the most powerful nation, the United States, can meet these challenges alone.

I have suggested a zone of international interest in the Persian Gulf to be declared by the United Nations and protected by its collective membership. This same principle can be applied more broadly. The U.S. government and security experts have identified the nation's critical infrastructure—generally agreed to include energy production and distribution systems, integrated financial systems, national communications systems, and our air, sea, and land transportation systems—which forms the core of our economic well-being, which is the national backbone on which other industries depend, and which could cause enormous economic and social damage if disrupted or seriously damaged. In this age of globalization, the same is increasingly true of the wider international world.

America's energy, banking, communications, and transportation systems are all increasingly integrated into those of almost all other developed nations. A single weapon of mass destruction in any one of several dozen major international seaports, especially if accompanied by threats to others, could virtually shut down the world's economy. There is an emerging international critical infrastructure that must be brought under the protection of an international security shield.

Therefore, the United States should take the lead in organizing international security forces to direct special protection to those facilities around the world upon which global communications, banking, energy, and transportation depend. Not every nation has the resources to protect all of its vital facilities, such as key seaports, gateway telecommunications switches, major oil refineries and depots, major tunnels, computer centers for international banking, and many dozens more. Protection of these critical facilities should increasingly become an international responsibility. A new security organization might be called, for example, the International Critical Infrastructure Protection Agency, and all major powers could contribute regular and special forces to its protective operations.

In large and small ways, the issue of national sovereignty will dominate the international and domestic political debates in the coming decades. As fundamental questions of governance become increasingly international, the United States and other states will be faced with a repeating dilemma: Do we ignore the problem? Do we seek to solve it ourselves? Or do we create institutions with others and give them sufficient authority to act? In dozens if not hundreds of instances, the ability of nations to solve common problems will depend on their willingness to cede a degree of their sovereignty to new international organizations in an effort to establish political coherence on the global commons. The issue of sovereignty is at the heart of the future of a new commonwealth of security.

The case for a reformed twenty-first-century United Nations was recently made in terms very similar to those presented here by one of its senior executives, Mark Malloch Brown, chief of staff to the U.N. secretary-general, who wrote that there is

> the broader challenge of aligning a too-often sprawling, unfocused UN system around today's priorities. A consequence of globalization that has crept up on all of us is that *our security is shared*. Poverty in one corner of the world can contribute to terrorism in another. From health pandemics to migration and global warming,

today's problems do not respect borders. A new multilateral compact is needed urgently but it will be effective only if it makes all of us—rich and poor—feel safer. [emphasis added][6]

This U.N. veteran's assessment is precisely the point: In a globalized world, borders offer few if any real protections, and the hope of security rests in creating both a shield and a cloak for the global commons. Given leadership, imagination, and this sense of the global commons, there is no reason that we cannot witness the same kind of burst of international cohesion created by the Trumans, Marshalls, Achesons, Monnets, Churchills, and many others in the mid-twentieth century. The times require it.

The Ladder of Hope

In many ways, America's security will depend on our ability to create hope among the hopeless. There are many ways to approach the undeveloped world, but two seem to dominate, and those two very much flow from an individual's cosmology. For those predestinarians who see mass poverty as endemic, a given in the human panoply, an unavoidable fact of life, little can or even should be done to alleviate the conditions of those who have drawn a low number in life's lottery. So it is written, so let it be.

For others, nothing is "written." Progress can be made in lifting even the most impoverished, and every effort should be made to do so. Those in the latter camp will continue to try, and the issue is whether there are better ways to try.[7] Those in the former camp will resist any notion of a comprehensive approach to hopelessness. Their

---

6. Mark Malloch Brown, "Why the UN Must Reinvent Itself or Collapse," *Sunday Times News Review*, February 20, 2005.

7. It has never been clear to me why many people seem born into one camp or the other and few change sides during their lives.

notice of poverty generally occurs only when the poor decide to do something about it and rise up.

There is the hope that a new consensus might form around the notion of direct connections among terrorism, fundamentalist revolution, tribal violence, and failed states and the stability and security of the United States and its allies. If the world is shrinking, as it seems to be, if trouble in far-off lands can eventually visit our shores in one way or another, attention must be paid. Those whose humanitarian instinct is not foremost may be persuaded that offering hope in concrete fashion may be more cost effective than preemptive wars, preventive invasions, and costly occupations and nation building.

A critique of traditional international development programs and projects is, once again, beyond the scope of this inquiry. Given that most of these programs are multinational, institution to nation, or nation to nation, they have been by and large top-down, that is to say, they have mostly consisted of financial grants and loans to governments with varying degrees of lender oversight.

The newer grassroots or community-based approach offers much appeal. This is direct assistance to individuals and local communities in small amounts that are project specific; in the case of individuals, they can be low-interest, long-term loans for the purchase of a loom, a taxi, a market stall, a cow, or even a mobile phone, and in the case of a local community, they can be loans for a new water well, a sanitation system, a clinic, a school, a telephone exchange, or any one of a hundred elementary needs. This is usually referred to as microlending, and in places like Bangladesh and Peru, it has often yielded amazing results, transforming the lives of people and communities.

The point here is not to design or redesign a new international aid program. It is to draw a connection between systemic underdevelopment and global unrest and insecurity. Creative minds can devise myriad ways of addressing the problems, but they must be addressed if the global commons is to be secure. In an age where a hundred al Qaedas are recruiting in the refugee camps, favelas, and urban slums of the world, where at least some of the insurgents blowing up American troops in Iraq come from a world of hopelessness and neglect, where teenage Palestinian women become suicide bombers, neglect is not an option. Any sane notion of security demands that attention be paid and action be taken.

Counterproliferation on the Commons

Much of early twenty-first-century insecurity arises from the confluence of technology, weapons of mass destruction, and the rise of the nonstate actor. That is to say, the ability to kill a lot of people now rests in the hands of more and more people accountable to no one. This may be a difficult case to make to a nation in which a hundred million citizens own at least that many guns. Nevertheless, it is a new reality. It is the problem of proliferation. And it forms the basis for much of this century's insecurity. Americans have been unable to reach consensus on gun control in part because of the argument that if private gun ownership is restricted, "only criminals will own guns."

To extend this argument logically to the international arena would be to say that all nations must have stockpiles of weapons of mass destruction, otherwise only nonstate actors will have them. The policy of the U.S. government, since the secret of nuclear weapons production spread to Russia and elsewhere, has been otherwise: The only security available must be through negotiated limits on the numbers of weapons possessed by members of the nuclear club and international restrictions on other nations joining the club.

What do we do when new nations such as North Korea or Iran join the nuclear club? In Asia, we are wisely seeking the help of China, Russia, Japan, and others to contain North Korea's threat and to seek elimination of its weapons-production capabilities. Likewise, in the Middle East, we are depending, at least for the moment, on the International Atomic Energy Agency to create an enforceable barrier between peaceful and military nuclear uses in Iran. However, the cat continues to struggle to escape the bag in other nations, such as Brazil, which see no justifiable reason that they too should not join the club. Insidiously, some nations now see in the different approaches that the United States has taken toward the nuclear nation of North Korea and the nonnuclear nation of Iraq a powerful argument to obtain a nuclear capability, as assurance against a U.S. invasion, as quickly as possible.

The United States, acting alone or with filmy "coalition forces," cannot invade every nation suspected of spinning its own centrifuge to enrich uranium. Therefore, to keep the cat in the bag will require American political partnership more than military force. The security of the commons can only be guaranteed by expanded and strengthened international shields against nuclear, biological, and chemical weapons production, strong inspection regimes, and effective sanctions on rogues and violators. Though this truth cuts directly across an increasingly unilateralist U.S. foreign policy, it is the truth nevertheless.

A Peace-Making Force

This suggests a wider role for international law enforcement as part of a security shield. Terrorists with weapons of mass destruction may represent the most urgent danger in the world, but they do not represent the only danger in the world. Tribal violence, ethnic nationalism, failed and fragile states, suicidal fundamentalism, drug cartels, and clans, gangs, and mafias—all are old phenomena and new, post–Cold War realities. No effective, established mechanism to respond to them now exists. The difference between peace keeping and peace making must be underscored.[8]

8. See Gary Hart, *The Fourth Power: A New Grand Strategy for the United States in the 21st Century* (New York: Oxford University Press, 2004), and other works by the author.

Peace keepers, now identified primarily with the United Nations, are defensively trained and equipped, that is, to be able to maintain the peace. They are not trained and equipped for offensive missions in combat zones. To *make* the peace, to force hostilities to cease in a combat environment, requires forces that are offensively trained, equipped, and experienced to suppress violence in an increasingly prevalent style of warfare: low-intensity conflict in urban environments. Even then, however, the best trained and equipped ground forces in the world, the U.S. Army, Marines, and Special Forces, cannot always easily prevail against indigenous insurgents, as we discovered in Mogadishu and are currently discovering in the cities of central Iraq.

We are learning lessons every day in Iraq, painful, bloody, and costly lessons, that may help in the (hopefully) unlikely possibility that we are tempted to attempt preemptive warfare in the future. But so are the insurgents. Like army ants, they pick and probe at soft spots, such as lightly armored Humvees, and use unconventional methods, such as kidnappings and civilian shields, to take advantage of our cultural values to defeat us. Their aim? To inflict enough casualties to cause the American people to conclude that there is no end to this.

Is there an alternative? Not one that will solve the problem of Iraq. But there is one that will reduce the burden on the United States. That is to create a standing international peace-making force in which the United States leads and participates. This will not happen without us; it may not happen even with us. But we should try. Member nations of the United Nations could provide designated and rotating military units, serving under international direction as approved by the Security Council, to a new force that is part constabulary and part special forces. It could be inserted into zones of violence to make the peace and then, once successful, withdrawn in favor of peace keepers and diplomatic negotiators. It must be trained and equipped for these missions and particularly it must train jointly, have common communications systems, and use interoperable weapons systems. National units may have their own national officers, but there would be an international command structure to supervise deployments and operations.

This force, composed of military units from member U.N. nations and serving under international officers, would be trained and equipped to impose peace in venues such as Rwanda, Haiti, Somalia, Kosovo, the Sudan, and elsewhere where genocide, tribal violence, or civil war threaten international peace and stability. Clearly, considerable thought would have to be given to the definition of what kinds of violence warrant international intervention as well as to the process for committing peace makers. This capability cannot be so passive as to be ineffective, nor can it be so aggressive as to impose its will arbitrarily. At the very least, deployment of U.N. peace makers should require Security Council approval, either the Security Council as presently constituted or as expanded and reformed.

From an American perspective, this idea has a number of advantages. The United States would be less tempted to go it alone or to intervene unilaterally. On the other hand, domestic political resistance to foreign involvement would be partly circumvented by the international community assuming responsibility. Moral indignation on the part of the United States and others would have an effective, ready-to-use outlet. The costs in lives and money would be more equally shared with other nations rather than being disproportionately borne by the United States. Renegade states, brutal dictators, violent tribal leaders, and international pirates would know there is a cop on the block with the power to suppress violence almost on a moment's notice. Such an international peace-making force would not be authorized to impose political settlements, but would simply halt violence. It would be for the diplomats and peace keepers to help work out political resolutions among indigenous conflicting forces.

The idea of international peace making faces a number of substantial obstacles, not least the problem of national sovereignty. Would the United States and other nations cede to the United

Nations part of their right to determine when war should or should not be waged? Would U.S. forces serve under foreign officers? What if the Security Council failed to act and, as in Rwanda and Darfur, hundreds of thousands of people continued to be slaughtered? Would a negative determination by the Security Council preclude individual nations, including the United States, from intervening?

Obviously, a large number of questions are required to be answered. But, as with arms-control negotiations, talk costs little, and it occasionally yields tangible results. This proposal illustrates yet again the degree to which globalization and the information revolution are bringing the world closer together and, at the same time, it recognizes eroding nation-state authority and state failure.

Another alternative to this suggestion would be for NATO to organize a peace-making force. In a de facto fashion, it is already doing so. Currently, NATO has approximately eight thousand troops in Afghanistan both making and keeping the peace. It is operating a modest training mission in Iraq. And it shares a common airborne warning and control system (AWACS) funded by its original thirteen member nations. The North Atlantic Treaty Organization is in the process of creating a NATO Response Force of about twenty thousand troops deployable in fewer than thirty days and in some cases as few as five days for rapid intervention, peace making and peace keeping, emergency relief, and training missions.

This is a historic departure from NATO's traditional culture of static territorial defense. The top commander of NATO, U.S. Marine Corps general James Jones, said in 2005 that the use of this force will require the reorganization of the ways in which NATO members finance such operations, but "if you build a NATO Response Force of 18,000 to 20,000 men, then you can actually use it to do something," such as the missions just described.[9]

9. Judy Dempsey, "Top General Seeks Radical Overhaul of NATO's Finances," *International Herald Tribune*, February 15, 2005.

A serious barrier to these notions is the familiar issue of national sovereignty. Though there would be nations that would willingly cooperate in such a new project to suppress violence in the world, there would be substantial political resistance to this approach in the United States. This is to be expected. It should be countered, however, by this question: In opposing an international peace-making force, are you therefore prepared either to leave violence unattended and our security potentially threatened, or to rely on the passage of time while ad hoc coalitions of the willing are being formed and danger mounts? Or do you wish to have the United States be the sole cop on the block to protect the security of the commons?

If our security shield is increasingly indivisible, the task of guaranteeing it should be shared.

America's role in the world of the twenty-first century must be to lead the reform of existing international institutions and to use our creativity to devise new ones to address new realities and challenges; to increase the world's attention to conditions of hopelessness and devise new direct ways of offering hope to individuals and communities; to dramatically increase international efforts to prevent the spread of weapons of mass destruction and the technologies that produce them; and to lead in the creation of a new international peace-making force.

The security of the commons requires this new role.

The New Warriors

In our own defense and in order to collaborate with like-minded peaceful nations to assure the security of the commons, the United States will require the shield of substantial military power. Its scale and scope and, most of all, its qualities and characteristics will be dictated by the new realities we face. The American military of the twenty-first century may evolve into something much different from the military of the twentieth century. Over the course of the last decade, a consensus formed among military thinkers that the post–Cold War construct used to determine force structures—the ability to fight two major theater wars (Persian Gulf and Korean peninsula) simultaneously—is no longer a dependable or useful guide. The potential for major regional wars is declining, and the reality of multiple smaller-scale conflicts is rising. The current U.S. administration recognized this in January 2005 when it announced the beginning of a reassessment of its force structures and types. It suggested a much greater emphasis in coming years on rapid deployment, rapid insertion expeditionary forces that are lighter, faster, and deployable in units smaller than the traditional division.

To protect ourselves and help to secure the global commons, the United States will require the full-scale adoption of maneuver warfare as its operational doctrine, the creation of a new human intelligence corps, the creation of a combined special forces capability as a fifth service, and a National Guard newly trained for the homeland security mission.

The Strategy of Maneuver

The military reform movement of the early 1980s, founded on the ideas of John Boyd and introduced thereafter into congressional military thinking, strongly urged U.S. military strategists to adopt maneuver warfare into our doctrine and operations. The U.S. Marine Corps did so overwhelmingly during that period, and some younger army officers promoted these ideas as well. There still lingers in the minds of some older officers and traditional theorists the sense that America's military superiority will triumph by sheer size and weight against any foreseeable foe. Old ideas and customs die hard.

Changing reality has a way of intruding on custom, however, and the new conflicts of the late twentieth and early twenty-first centuries have reduced the importance of mass and firepower and increased the importance of speed, agility, flexibility, innovation, and surprise. This is shaping the thinking and practice of those who identify these trends as fourth-generation warfare, or low-intensity conflict increasingly involving insurgents and nonstate actors. The current administration's rather slow and reluctant acceptance of the new realities of warfare and the reforms needed to adapt to them are welcome late rather than not at all.

As part of a new approach to the military component of national and global commons security, the concept of maneuver warfare should represent all of those changes in operational doctrine, force structures, weapons procurement, and types of forces required to prevail in the age of fourth-generation warfare. In the twenty-first century, the doctrine of maneuver warfare is less an operational doctrine and more a way of thinking, a new kind of security shield created by creative thought and imagination.

A Human Intelligence Corps

Before the age of high technologies—long-range listening devices, sophisticated signals intelligence collection, high-resolution cameras in satellites, and a stunning myriad of mind-bending ways to vacuum up massive amounts of data—intelligence collection, spying, was done primarily by human beings. This old-fashioned method of learning secrets is still called Humint for human intelligence collection. Except in rare penetrations of the Soviet Union involving human sources, much of Humint in the Cold War was carried out in foreign embassies around the world. It has always been important. But if you can track the comings and goings of the Soviet submarine fleet leaving from and arriving back into port from a hundred miles in space, the importance of getting a Soviet sailor drunk in a saloon in Amsterdam is diminished in importance.

Now the age of terrorism, with its more complex security chess board, has dramatically changed all that. The most super-sophisticated satellite cameras in the world with the most incredibly precise camera resolutions have been scouring the mountain ranges along the Afghanistan-Pakistan border for about three years now looking for Osama bin Laden and have not found him. Without doubt, the most sensitive sound-detection devices known to man have been trying, likewise without avail, to hear him. If he is ever found, it will be most likely because the friend of a nephew of a herdsman or caravan driver drops a hint to an acquaintance in a souk in a town in northwestern Pakistan and it is overheard by a clever employee of the Central Intelligence Agency who has learned the language and knows how to work the street or who obtains the information from one of his carefully cultivated local sources.

The odds will be greatly improved if that CIA agent is a Pakistani American who can look, speak, and live the part of a local. Right now, we don't have nearly enough of them because we spent our money over the years on those satellites. To remedy this, we should create an elite human intelligence corps within the CIA that would reestablish the primacy of the individual human being over technology. Arab-American young people, not Anglo Americans, should be the priority recruits. If they have traveled in their parents' land of origin and speak the language, even better. Otherwise, if they are clever and dedicated enough, the foreign language and culture can be learned. Selection for this corps should signal membership in a new intelligence elite and be a steppingstone to senior intelligence advancement. Some experience in human intelligence collection should be required of all those given senior agency positions. In a word, human intelligence should be restored to the central role that its importance now requires in forming a shield of security.

The Fifth Service

The warfare of the twenty-first century now requires us to consider the consolidation of the special forces of the individual services into a fifth branch of the armed forces, joining the army, navy, marine corps, and air force. The U.S. Air Force itself did not exist during World War II. It was created, as were the Department of Defense and the Central Intelligence Agency, by the National Security Act of 1947 as a new fourth military service.

As conditions required it, the army and navy developed special forces capabilities: in the army the Rangers and Delta Force, in the navy the SEALS. One could argue that in its style of operations and esprit the marine corps is a large special force. And the air force itself has small units capable of insertion, interdiction, rescue, and special operations. The question is whether the remarkable capabilities that these organizations represent should remain primarily with their individual services and be secondarily available for joint operations, or whether they should primarily operate jointly as their own service and be secondarily available to their services of origin.

Special forces capabilities must multiply. By their very nature and the nature of their missions, they will never be organized in large units. But they will increasingly be called upon to form the frontline of operations in foreign conflicts, replacing the conventional large-unit combat forces that crossed the beaches of Normandy and that fought up and down the Korean peninsula. Vietnam saw the reemergence of small-unit combat, and the conflicts of the late twentieth century, save for the Iraqi invasion, followed this trend. The question is whether there will be more Iraqi-style national invasions or more small conflicts requiring highly specialized capabilities. If the trend is toward the latter, relying on the loan of special forces from two or three services on an ad hoc basis will probably not suffice. Therefore, consideration should be given to regularizing their joint operations under a single new command.

The existing services will resist, as the army did when faced with seeing its air corps peeled away to form the U.S. Air Force. It is in the nature of human organizations, particularly military ones, to resist giving up what they have. But this proposal merits serious discussion ahead of the time when the requirement for a single special forces command is called for on a continuing basis.

Steps in this direction have already been taken. An assistant secretary of defense has been designated to coordinate resources for the special forces, and they are increasingly thought of as a separate force for strategic planning purposes. This proposal is to make formal what reality is already forcing as a practical proposition.

The National Guard

For a brief moment in his speech of September 20, 2001, President Bush, echoing President Kennedy forty years before, called upon Americans to pull together and to help each other and the nation, to themselves find ways to strengthen, protect, and serve their country. That message has not been heard since. The National Guard is both a vehicle and a model for national service in the age of insecurity. Its ranks must be replenished and expanded if it is to be the backbone of homeland security, but it must be tasked with that mission and quickly. This will fulfill the will of the nation's founders, who included these mandates in the U.S. Constitution:

> Article I, sec. 8: [The Congress shall have the power] To provide for Calling forth the Militia to execute the Laws of the Union, suppress insurrections and repel Invasions. To provide for organizing, arming, and disciplining, the Militia, and for governing such Part of them as may be employed in the Service of the United States;

> Article II, sec. 2: The President shall be Commander in Chief of the Army and Navy of the United States, and of the Militia of the several States, when called into the Service of the United States;

THE SECURITY OF THE COMMONS

Amendment II: A well regulated Militia, being necessary to the security of a free State, the right of the people to keep and bear Arms, shall not be infringed.[10]

At this point in America's long history, it seems important to note, once again, the wisdom of the founders. Did they anticipate terrorist warfare on American soil in the early twenty-first century? Of course not. But they did anticipate that the United States would be vulnerable to some kinds of attack for quite some time and that an army of citizen-soldiers that did not threaten republican freedoms and constitutional liberties would be necessary. Here it is. Except, the National Guard is not here. It is in Iraq. The danger to American security is here, not in Iraq. The Constitution says nothing about the militia/National Guard invading or occupying foreign nations. The army required by the Constitution to "repel Invasions" is not here to repel terrorist invasions, nor is it being trained and equipped to do so. Any clear reading of the U.S. Constitution in this regard can only conclude that the commander in chief and those subordinate to him, by extended foreign deployment of the primary homeland defenders, are guilty of dereliction of their duty to protect the homeland. Further, extended, seemingly endless deployments of National Guard units are causing serious problems in recruitment for the National Guard and in retention of those in National Guard service.

The age of terrorism now requires us to use the National Guard for its intended purpose, thereby increasing citizen security and, at the same time, to use it as a model of other ways in which to empower all citizens to participate in providing their own security and that of their neighborhoods, communities, and nation. The threat of terrorism thus offers an opportunity to revitalize the American republic.

10. Constitution of the United States.

The U.S. Commission on National Security/21st Century and the Council on Foreign Relations task force that followed a year after 9/11 both concluded that the National Guard of the fifty states must play a central role in preventing terrorist attacks on the United States and in responding to them if they should occur. The principal reasons for this conclusion are constitutional and practical. The U.S. Constitution recognizes the militia of the several states, now called the National Guard, as a counterpart of the regular or standing forces and as the frontline of defense of the homeland. The reasons for this rest in twenty-five hundred years of republican theory that holds that regular forces deployed in a republic are a threat to liberty, and the defense of the republic is best left in the hands of citizen-soldiers. And practically, as citizen-soldiers, members of the National Guard are "forward deployed," that is, they are resident on a daily basis in all of the cities and towns across America and therefore readily available and on call for duty with very little mass transport or relocation.

National Guard units cannot carry out the homeland security mission unless they are trained and equipped for it, activities that have yet to occur. In large part, this has not occurred because large numbers of National Guardsmen and women are currently deployed in Iraq. Additionally, a disproportionate number of members of the National Guard are also first responders, that is, police officers, firefighters, hazardous-material teams, and emergency health workers. So, by their presence in Iraq, they make America doubly vulnerable. They are not guarding the homeland or preparing to respond to terrorism wearing either their first-responder hats or their National Guard hats.

The genuine security of the American commons urgently requires the return of foreign-deployed National Guard members and their training and equipping for their roles and missions as a homeland security shield. Until this happens, the United States will be more vulnerable to terrorist attacks than it need be and less capable of dealing with the aftermath of attacks than it must be.

The new warriors will be composed of a redesigned National Guard with a vital homeland security mission, military forces trained to think in maneuver terms for fourth-generation warfare, an elite human intelligence collection corps capable of swimming in any stream in the world, and a new consolidated special forces command as the cutting edge in virtually all future expeditionary operations.

A New National Security Policy

The national security policy of the United States in the early twenty-first century, combining cloak and shield, must incorporate the transformation of the U.S. economy, a new role for the United States in the world, and a new approach to military and intelligence organizations and training.

Our security is inseparable from the security of others. In the twenty-first century, more than ever, there will be strength in numbers. The wider the net of those sharing the security of the commons, the more isolated the forces of destruction and disintegration will become. There is neither security in isolation nor security in preventive invasions. The United States, like all other nations, reserves the right of preemption, as it always has, for those circumstances where a state or group of nonstate actors presents a clear and present danger, established by flawless intelligence, and a threat that is immediate and unavoidable. But we should not use ambitions of empire, cloaked in aggressive rhetoric and false fears, to justify the invasion of other nations. When we hammer our shield into a spear without just cause, we are less rather than more secure.

If our national security policy today is war on terrorism using primarily military means, what would victory in that war or, more accurately, those wars actually entail? One persuasive scenario of the world after the preemptive or preventive invasion of Iraq, the bombing of Iran, the reduction of North Korea, and similar imperial undertakings has been provided by Michael Howard, the British military historian. From the perspective of a believer in the classic American republic, it is not an inviting one:

> Ultimately, the United States would have once again, as after the Second World War, to assume the burden of building and maintaining peace on the foundations of the wars it had won. This could mean converting its hegemony into something more resembling an empire; taking up the Kipling-esque burden of policing the defeated territories and leading them, in spite of their protests, "toward the light" of Western-style modernization. Like all empires, it would have to police its turbulent periphery, but unlike its predecessors it would still remain vulnerable to catastrophic blows to its centre. Such responsibilities, with all their attendant obligations, are not likely to appeal to the people of the United States.[11]

America cannot be at once an empire and a republic. The principles of the American republic, to which we pledge our allegiance, upon which our Constitution is based, and upon which our nation was founded are our greatest power and surest guide. The strength of our civic nationalism, when we actually choose to exercise it, offers hope to the world. When these core civic values become a more harsh and aggressive nationalism, we lose our moral authority and the great strength of our principles, and we sacrifice the cloak of security.

11. Michael Howard, *The Invention of Peace and the Reinvention of War* (London: Profile, 2001), pp. 123–124.

Conclusion

Security's Web

Freedom requires security. An insecure individual or an insecure nation cannot be said to be truly free. The freedom of every American and the freedom of the United States itself are dependent on the degree of security we can achieve. This equation is complicated by the belief on the part of some that the way to achieve security is to take away at least some degree of freedom. They believe that some freedoms must be sacrificed in order to achieve security. This is becoming the central issue in the struggle to understand the true nature of security in the twenty-first century.

All civilized societies, including the United States, have recognized that certain rules are required to maintain a civil society. Everyone is not at liberty to do exactly as he or she wishes. All kinds of restrictions, from driver's licenses to zoning ordinances, are placed on our conduct as individuals by laws and regulations required to promote the common good. There is always an ongoing debate about how much freedom must be forgone to make society function in an orderly way. In many cases, Americans differ from other civilized societies. We permit our citizens to possess deadly weapons on a scale virtually unknown in the rest of the world, yet we regulate what scenes and language can be included in movies more than almost any other democratic nation. Our differences in the powers we do and do not grant to the state to regulate citizen behavior flow from our culture and our history, and even that understanding of our true cultural values shifts and changes from age to age.

In this age of terror, as during certain stages of the Cold War, we have enacted laws, such as the Patriot Act particularly, that give the state greater powers to intrude on our lives and thus to restrict our freedoms in the name of security. Those favoring such laws have traditionally been those most critical of government's powers. Congress has authorized agents of the state to search our homes and offices without judicial warrants. We have especially empowered the government to take harsh measures against anyone it thinks might be aiding and abetting terrorist organizations.

This has led to the incarceration of "detainees" without limits of time or due process, the shameful behavior of troops in the uniform of the United States brutalizing Iraqi prisoners, and the notorious prisons at Guantanamo Bay, Cuba, and elsewhere in locations we are not even told about. The degree to which all this, done by our government in the name of national security, violates the Constitution and laws of the United States, not to say also international law, will be determined in the coming months and years by the American judiciary. As we seek a greater security shield, however, it is safe to say we have all sacrificed some degree of the cloak of our freedom. Though these new intrusive powers of government may make some feel more secure, they do not feel that way to me.

The balance between security and freedom is neither an absolute nor an easy one. We do not think about it much in times of calm. When insecurity increases or our safety is threatened, however, serious questions of what we value most come into play. How much freedom will we give up to achieve how much security? How much freedom do we give up to achieve security before we are no longer what we claim to be, a democracy based on constitutional processes? It is one of the many curiosities of politics that those who claim to value liberty and freedom the most are often the first to want to take them away—or perhaps just to take them away from other people whom they do not like or trust. It turns out that it is not liberty and freedom as universal principles but *their* liberty and freedom that they wish to protect.

During one of America's periods of greatest insecurity, the Great Depression, when many people wondered whether our nation could actually hold together, in his January 1941 State of the Union speech President Franklin Roosevelt proposed his famous four freedoms: freedom from fear, freedom from want, freedom of speech, and freedom of worship. By doing so, he implicitly identified the enemies of freedom as fear, deprivation, oppression, and intolerance. Fear and want were the sources of the greatest insecurity for Americans as well as for others who also could not speak or worship as they chose. As in those days, now our greatest enemy is fear itself. Roosevelt understood that genuine security was inextricably linked to freedom and that freedom from fear was not simply freedom from fear of violence, but it was also freedom from want and hunger and it was freedom from a sense of being unwanted and left behind.

Terrorism causes fear, therefore we must rid ourselves of terrorism. But if by miracle or simple persistence, we were to rid ourselves of terrorism, would we then be secure? Or would there be other causes of fear and therefore insecurity? The loss of the means of livelihood is the source of fear for many. Potential harm from environmental poison or climate change is the source of fear for many. For millions of forgotten elderly citizens, inadequate nutrition, health care, and medicine are the causes of great fear and insecurity. It is the source of considerable wonder that those most eager to sacrifice some freedoms to create a shield, or spear, against terrorism are unwilling to demonstrate equal zeal in attacking other sources of insecurity in order to create a cloak of security.

America will not be truly secure, or free from fear, until we undertake to address the multiple sources of insecurity. This will require us to think differently about who we truly are and what our values, and therefore our priorities, truly are. If freedom is the product of security, then we must create a new understanding of security in the twenty-first century much as Franklin Roosevelt did in the twentieth century. Our new four freedoms should be freedom of the commons, freedom of livelihood, freedom of a sound environment, and freedom from fear. Around this nucleus, a number of other freedoms might also be added.

Assume for a moment that the last terrorist on earth has been captured. We will all breathe a great sigh of relief. There will quite probably be a memorial service at the site of the World Trade Center which will combine grief with joy. Having that threat removed, we will without doubt feel much more secure. But certain insecurities, fears, and therefore restrictions on our freedom will remain. Should we not also address them and determine whether even greater security might be available to all Americans over and above freedom from the fear of terrorism?

As we did during the Cold War, even now during the war on terrorism we are in danger of defining our security too narrowly as simply a military shield, and therefore we may also be in danger of selling ourselves and our nation short. If terrorism has simply replaced communism, and before it fascism, as the external threat that causes us to unite for the time being until a victory is won and then we will return to "ordinary" life full of its own insecurities, we will have missed a window of opportunity as a nation to consider what American security in this new century should truly mean.

The new world we now inhabit will not continue to permit us to believe that we can keep threats to our security in distant realms. The real meaning of 9/11 is that America is vulnerable, vulnerable not just to suicidal terrorists but also to economic and political tides that now wash up on our shores in ways that Americans have never experienced before. In many ways, these tides are great sources of insecurity in that they disrupt the ways in which we are accustomed to living. But, given imagination and creativity, they might also hold great opportunity and promise for a new kind of security cloak. The key in our continuing search for more perfect security is to know that security, like freedom, is indivisible. International security, national security, and community security all share this common fact: If any of us is insecure, then in varying degrees all of us share that insecurity.

Despite its great power, the United States neither could nor should prevent other nations, including China and Russia, from succeeding and growing. Indeed, there is no stronger deterrent to war than a ringing cash register. And increased economic interdependence reduces the likelihood of conflict. For other nations to succeed, it is not necessary for the United States to decline or fail. It should be our goal in our search for a new kind of security to expand the number of nations that have a stake in the United States being secure by helping them to create protections for themselves. We can do much better at defining our interests in ways that provide benefits for others. In the twenty-first century, neither isolation nor empire is an option for the United States.

Somewhere among these ideas—the republican ideal of civic virtue, the sense of commonwealth and the common good, and an American civic nationalism that is internationalist—rest the secrets to achieving security's shield and cloak. *We are all in this together* is one of the usual ways of articulating these notions. We must all pull together, or we will all pull apart. There is no security in pulling apart, so we better pull together.

A republic of security, at whose center is the security of the commons, should be our goal. Without idealizing either the flawed Greek city-state or the equally problematic Roman republic, there are at the core of their creation profound truths important to our twenty-first-century search for security. These include the sense that citizenship in the U.S. republic carries with it certain duties and obligations, that among those duties is shared concern for the security of the republic, that some citizens cannot be insecure and therefore not free without all being insecure and therefore not free, and that there are common goods and the commonwealth—what today we call the national interest.

The national interest today begins and ends with the promise of security, but it is a sense of security that extends beyond simply the defeat of terrorism. If America's insecurities are increasingly experienced in common, then we have a common interest in reducing those insecurities. And if the many global insecurities are being experienced by Americans due to our increasing participation in an international commons, then we have common interest with the peoples of many nations in reducing the insecurities we all are feeling.

Pulling together in the new century will require a reaffirmation of our core beliefs, the principles upon which our republic and its systems of government are based, what has been called the American creed:

> The essential elements of the American Creed and
> American civic nationalism are faith in liberty, constitu-
> tionalism, the law, democracy, individualism and cultural
> and political egalitarianism. They have remained in
> essence the same through most of American history.
> They are chiefly rooted in the Enlightenment and are
> also derived from English traditions: the liberal philoso-
> phy of John Locke as well as much older beliefs in the
> law and in "the rights of freeborn Englishmen."[1]

In the rapidly internationalizing world of the twenty-first century, there are increasing numbers of forces, what Michael Howard calls the "lateral pressures of globalization," aided by far-flung com-

---

1. Anatol Lieven, *America Right or Wrong: An Anatomy of American National-ism* (New York: Oxford University Press, 2004), p. 49.

munications networks competing for our loyalty. These new communities separate from the state include religious missions and ethnic identities, international human rights organizations, and women's rights groups. There are environmental causes, such as climate change, global warming, and ocean protection. Perhaps most significant, people are finding identity in their affiliation with transnational professional organizations, financial networks, and global corporations. Because of these transnational loyalties and especially new commercial identities, according to Howard, "the national flag is no longer a symbol to evoke awe and respect. At best it is the logo of a firm . . . whose function is to provide dividends for its shareholders."[2] When the American flag becomes merely a commercial logo, a patch to be put on our products, the reason to die for it will have long since disappeared.

My search for a new sense of national security is in fact a search for a new sense of civic patriotism, a new belief—or perhaps the restoration of an old belief—in an ideal of national unity. The lessons I have learned from thirty years of searching for the elusive nature of security and the means for achieving it shape my sense that the Cold War years shrunk our notion of security and diminished its true nature and because of that may be leading us astray from this American creed and the kind of international leadership by principled example advocated by John Quincy Adams.

Seventy years ago, Franklin Roosevelt was closer to a true understanding of security and the American creed than we are today. If security really is freedom from fear, then eliminating only one source of fear, albeit an important one, does not guarantee the protection of a cloak of security to which *every* American is entitled.

With the transformation of the nature of security must come a transformation of the means for rescuing us from insecurity. We

2. Michael Howard, *The Invention of Peace and the Reinvention of War* (London: Profile, 2001), p. 100.

cannot know how to achieve security unless we know what security means, what it is that we are truly after. Security cannot be bought by the sacrifice of freedom. And there is an increasing sense that almost every threat has on its other side, if we can just figure out how to view its other side, an opportunity. And quite often that opportunity represents the means for reducing if not eliminating the threat with which it is associated. A strategy for achieving security requires us to assess our powers—all our powers, not just our substantial military powers—and to think creatively about how to use our powers to take advantage of new opportunities to reduce and hopefully eliminate threats old and new.

How will we actually know when we are secure? some may ask. Like many public goods, security is difficult to measure. But I will suggest one possible standard: When every child in America is secure, then America will be secure. But this is an impossible task, you may say. I strongly disagree. The wealthiest and most powerful nation in the history of the world is capable of creating a cloak of security for all of its children. We have the means; we have the resources. We only lack the political will. Every child in America can receive adequate nutrition, can be warmly sheltered, can receive all necessary medical care, can be provided a good education, and can be protected by family and society. Every child in America deserves and should receive all of these things. This goal is within the reach of our nation at the peak of its powers. This goal as a measure of our security is politically and economically achievable, and as a measure of our humanity it is necessary. Even more important, this goal is morally necessary. The national goal of security for our children is crucial to the security of the commons. What do we have more in common than a desire for the welfare and security of our children? Once we have brought all of America's children under a cloak of security, then we will be well on our way to achieving the security of the republic.

When we restore the ideal of the commons, the sense that security is both a shared obligation and a shared right, we will emerge from our individual, heavily fortified homes and castles into that commons and defy any threat, terrorist or otherwise, to defeat us. Because together we will be strong, we will be unbeatable, we will possess security's cloak and its shield.

For this is security's web.

Index